WALKING THE
REFUGE

Michael Allen George

WALKING THE
REFUGE

Printed in the United States of America.

Brilliant Books Literary
137 Forest Park Lane Thomasville
North Carolina 27360 USA

For
Tom and Bonnie Haubenschild
Without Them
It would be a mighty
lonely time

Books by Michael Allen George

The Refuge Mystery Series
Why A Refuge	Book One
Bridge for a lost refuge	Book Two
When Refuge Grass Was Greener	Book Three
To Save The Refuge	Book Four
Without Refuge	Book five
Refuge Of Another Kind	Book Six

Written as Michael Allen George
Places Of Refuge	Book Seven
Refuge Life And Home	Book Eight
Refuge Rescuers	Book Nine
Walking The Refuge	Book Ten

Books Written as Michael George
Horses Lemons And Pretty Girls
More Horses And Pretty Girls
Finding Peri Gray
Of Rain Barrels And Bridges

Books Written With Bud George And David George
Stories From Three Brothers
More Stories From Three Brothers

PROLOGUE

Dan Tucker lifted his hard hat off his head and set it on the floor next to his seat. He released his seat belt, stood, and climbed out of the D9 cat. He didn't like what he'd just seen while moving the fresh piles of garbage dumped the previous evening.

He used his gloved hands to move a large piece of cardboard out of the way and there it was. The body of what appeared to be a young, still healthy, German Shepard. He used its leg to pull it out of the pile. Whatever happened to it, it didn't in his opinion, deserved to be buried in a garbage dump. No animal as noble as a dog deserved that.

He dragged the body to a place it would be out of the way for the day. He would take it with him after work and find a proper place to bury it. He was about the get back on the D9 and go back to work when he heard a strange sound. It seemed to be coming from the pile he'd been moving onto the main pile.

Dan went back to his smaller pile and dug around some more. Only a small way down in the pile, he found a large cardboard box emitting the sound. Inside, he found four mixed breed pups. He guessed their age to be about a week. Three were still alive. Alive, but barely. He lay the dead pup next to the German Shepard, then carried the three live pups to the foreman's cage at the edge of the dump.

The foreman was a tough task master, and normally looked askance at any kind of extra break. Even a pee break. But he carried a soft spot for dogs. And like most people, he was especially fond of puppies. So as soon as he saw the pups, he filled a spare cup with water from the cooler that was always kept in his foreman's cage.

The pups couldn't drink on their own, so the two men used their fingers to get at least a small amount of water in the pups. The foreman also called the animal control people in the county, and explained the situation to them. They said they would sent someone out to pick up the pups.

The foreman kept watch on the pups and Dan went back to work on his D9. About an hour later, a person from animal control walked in front of the D9 and signaled for the Dan to stop.

"My name is Polly Lambert. I need to ask you some questions," she said.

"Fine," he answered. "But make them short. The foreman gets pissed anytime we stop working. He never cares the reason."

"I'll keep it simple. Why did you pick this way to get rid of those pups? There are three rescue facilities in this county who would have taken them in."

"Sorry, Ma'am," he said to the pretty young lady who very generously filled out the uniform she was wearing. "But it isn't me who's getting rid of those pups. It's the asshole who dumped them here who is."

"I find it hard to believe that anyone would just throw puppies into a dump. For one thing, it would be too easy to get caught."

"Whoever did it, did it at the end of the day. They were the last customer. We were already on our way out when they were here. The foreman handled the whole deal, and he never leaves his cage."

"That sounds convenient." Polly gave him what she considered her best frown. "But it also sounds like you're trying to cover your tracks. You should learn to treat animals better. They deserve decent treatment, just as much as we do."

"I'm well aware of that. What you don't know is what huge assholes most people can be. I've seen near everything you can imagine here, that some jackass or another dumped. So dumping some puppies ain't that unusual. And that ain't the only thing that was dumped yesterday." He point to the edge of the dump. "Over there is the body of a dog I found in this pile, before I found the pups. I figured I'd take it somewhere tonight and bury it. It sure didn't deserve to be just dumped here."

"Will you show me the body?"

"Why? Ain't a damn thing you can do for it now."

"I'm well aware of that. But part of my job is to investigate anything that might be cruelty to animals. If I can see the dog, maybe I can figure out what happened to it."

"Okay, but just so you know, I'm going to get my ass chewed for taking this much time with you."

He took her to the German Shepard. She examined the dogs eyes, looked into his ears and mouth, then sighed heavily. Shaking her head, she stood and faced him. "We'll be taking the body with us," she said "That dead pup too. So you won't have to worry about it."

"You going to tell me what the hell's going on?" Dan asked. "First you accuse me of trying to get rid of these pups. Now you're going to help me out by taking care of the dead dog. "I'd sure like to know why."

"I'm only doing my job. It's nothing to concern you. Just go back to work. We'll do what needs to be done."

"Does refusing to tell me what this is about make you feel important? Or do you just not like me because it's my fault for finding the pups and the dead dog?"

"Neither one," Polly claimed. "It's just not your concern. So go back to work and forget about this."

"That's not likely. You're making a mystery where there don't appear any need for one." Dan gave her the best evil eye he could come up with. It didn't scare her. "I hate mysteries," he added as he got back on the D9.

The incident bothered him all day, and he talked about it with the other guys from the dump when they stopped for their usual beer after work that night.

The consensus of opinion was that he was right. None of it made any sense at all. It continued to bother him throughout the evening, and even during the night.

When he went to work the next morning though, was when it really hit him. He started on a fresh pile again, dumped at the last minute the day before. As soon as the blade of the D9 hit it, it happened again. Something under the large sheet of cardboard. Another German Shepard. This one was a little older and scruffier. As in the dog the day before, he couldn't tell what had happened to it.

The foreman wasn't happy about the delay, but his own innate love of dogs forced to to agree to call animal control. The same two came again. The male stayed to interview the foreman, and the young lady went with Dan to the garbage pile.

"Before you get to pointing your finger at me again," he told her. "I want you to know, I only found the dog. I didn't do anything to hurt it. It was already dead."

"I"m not pointing fingers," she answered. "If you were trying to get rid of a dead dog, I know that D9 of yours would do a good job of it. So stop worrying."

Dan looked at the creases in her forehead and general frown covering her face. "I'll do that when you do," he said.

"Why would you say something like that?" she asked as she started her examination of the dog.

"The look on your face."

"So now you don't like my looks? After yesterday, I guess I don't blame you. I was out of line when I accused you of dumping the pups. I apologize for that."

"That's got nothing to do with it. It's the frown on your face that I'm talking about. The frown that's making a mystery out of all this."

And she did carry an extra large frown when she finished with the dog. She looked at the pile of garbage that still hadn't been moved up to the main pile. Being careful to not disturb the body of the dead dog, she started moving some more cardboard. It only took a short time to uncover the bodies of three more dogs. All of them Golden Retrievers. They were still in decent condition, so they obviously hadn't been dead for very long.

She took out her cell phone and dialed a number. She turned her back on Dan and walked away from him as she talked. When she returned, she told him that he was free to leave. The dump was now shut down for the day.

"Why," Dan asked her. "I know that whatever it is that happened to those dogs really sucks. I love dogs too. But shutting the dump down for the day because you found some dead ones? Makes no sense. You're creating a hardship for way too many people doing that. What the hell are all the garbage haulers supposed to do?"

"I don't know. We're just doing what we need to do."

"But, Jesus, this is going to raise hell with so many people and things. There's a lot more to this than just some garbage and dead dogs. There's a lot of people who's jobs are going to be royally screwed up by this move."

"I'm well aware of that. But there's not a damn thing I can do about it. Neither can you. So you might just as well check out and go home. I need to get to work. It's going to be a long enough day as it is."

It was too early in the day for anyone to stop for a beer, so Dan went home to think about what was going on. It was only a short time later when the headache started, that he acquired from the mystery he knew he had little chance of solving.

It stayed with him throughout the day and into the night. By morning it had eased up considerably, and with no new piles of garbage or dead dogs, it was gone by the end of the day. By the end of the week, he managed to rid himself of most of the haunting dog thoughts rattling his brain.

By Monday morning, he was almost looking forward to his usual boring day. Nothing but driving his D9 and pushing piles of garbage around. He was even relaxed enough to ignore the fact that there were three fresh piles of garbage to be moved. They were dumped there the last thing before closing on Saturday afternoon.

He fired up his cat and started his daily work of pushing garbage. He only managed to move the pile about six feet when what he saw in front of him shocked him enough to make him think he might have a heart attack. The tension he felt was so strong as he dismounted the D9 that he had a hard time doing it without falling.

He didn't have to move anything this time. The five bodies of several breeds of dogs were all right there. With a great deal of trepidation, he walked to the foreman's cage. When the foreman saw him coming with the look Dan carried on his face, his only question was, "How many?"

Polly was again the one who went with Dan to the five dogs. It only took a quick look at one of the dogs to start her head shaking. She took several deep breaths, dialed a number on her cell phone, and as before, she turned her back on Dan and walked away when her phone conversation started.

Dan knew then, that no matter what Polly or any of the animal control people did or told him, he was going to somehow get some answers.

This time, when they again shut the dump down, early in the day or not, all the guys stopped for a beer before going home. They were surprised a short time later when the foreman joined them.

"I know," he said, "that you guys might not like talking much with me around, but bear with me. I'm not up to going home just yet. Last time they shut us down, I didn't get out of there until early afternoon. That was still earlier than what I usually got there. My wife was doing her daily cleaning. She's a clean freak, and was pissed at me for interrupting her. We ended up having a nasty fight. I'm not up to going through that again today. If I'd a caught her in bed with someone, that wouldn't have been so bad. But damn, she can't do a damn thing normal."

For the first time, all of the guys became friends with the foreman before they quit and went home. They also decided that they had to change the way things were done in the dump at the end of the day. They agreed, they didn't need any more dead dogs.

And Dan decided, that no matter what else he did, he more than ever wanted to solve the mystery of the dogs. It was obvious that animal control wouldn't give him any answers.

CHAPTER 1

Mack and Lisa Thomas were on a pleasant walk in the Clayborne County Wildlife Refuge. They were on the last leg of their favorite trail. It made an eight mile loop, but had enough cross trails so a person could hike as short as a mile, or take the full eight miles. At this last half mile of the trail, it ran along the shore of Rice Lake. So named because of the large quantity of wild rice it produced every year.

The rice was harvested, but only in the old fashioned way. With canoes and paddles. The only people allowed to do the harvesting were kids, aged fourteen to eighteen. All of them were from special education classes. But they were a different mix than would be normally found in a group like that. Some were, as would be expected, kids with learning disabilities. However, there were those kids' all the way to kids so bright they were constantly bored with the normal school curriculum.

There were none of them there that day though. Harvest season was still months away. Instead, it was quiet as they walked. Natures type of quiet. Which was, other than the shuffle of their walking, no human sound. Even so, the air was filled with other sound, all of it soothing, rather than the blaring of motorized vehicles of all kinds. Horn and sirens. Electric saws and power nail guns. Screaming kids and barking dogs.

No. All they could hear was the life affirming song of birds. The busy insect hum. The gentle breeze flowing through the leaves. The occasional howl of a coyote, telling all how important they were.

They hadn't either, seen another person during what was for them a rather short walk. It was only the two of them, strolling through the crisp morning air. Holding hands, something they both loved to do, even after their shared years of marriage.

It was one of their better days, and if time would have allowed it, a day they would have stretched out much further. They were already beginning to feel the effects of something special nearing its end, when they rounded a bend in the trail. A man, waving his arms at them, was but a short distance away.

"I wonder," Mack said softly to Lisa, "what it is that he wants?"

"So do I," Lisa agreed. "And I'll bet that whatever it is, it can't be good."

"Are you Mack and Lisa Thomas?" Dan Tucker asked them as he closed the gap between them.

"We are," Mack answered. "What can we do for you?"

"You can go to work for me. You are detectives, right?"

"We are, but we normally talk to clients at the office. Which is open now. So why are you out here, looking for us?"

"I was at your office. I have no doubts about anyone there. I'm sure they are all good at what they do. But I came here to find you two because of your reputations. You are noted for your love for, and abilities with, animals of all types. That's why I want you to work for me, more than anyone else."

"Well," Mack told him, "we don't try to find lost dogs, or any other animal. There's a lot of ways you can do that on your own. We also avoid the usual cruelty cases. There are a lot of organizations who can deal with them better than we can."

"I don't want to hire you for anything like that. What I want is a lot more serious, I think. I came here to find you, instead of waiting at your office, because my boss doesn't like for me to take time off. I had to play hell with him just to get a few hours this morning. And the only reason I got this short a time off, is because he loves dogs as much as I do."

"Like Mack already told you," Lisa explained, "we don't do the normal animal cases."

"What I want you to do, isn't normal. Let me just explain what's happening. Then you'll see, this isn't normal. You see, I work at the Main Street Dump. A couple of weeks ago, I…" Dan went on the tell them about the pups and the German Shepard that started his mystery, then went completed his story. Finally he said, "and this last time. Just yesterday morning, I found more. After I saw them, I knew I had to find out what is going on. There were twenty-five that time. Twenty-five dead dogs. Small ones sure, but each and every one of them had some kind of a life. And it was somehow just snuffed out of them. It ain't fair. Somethings real wrong someplace. That's why I want to hire you. To find out what it is that's going on. I don't expect you to fix it. Only just tell me what the hell it's about."

"An investigation into something like that could get expensive," Mack said. "Are you sure you want to spend the money?"

"Yes. I don't have a lot of savings, but I'll spend all I have. And if that ain't enough, I can always remortgage my house."

"We would very much prefer," Lisa said, "that you don't carry it that far. It could easily cause you permanent problems."

"Maybe," Dan argued. "But if it could someway maybe stop whoever it is that's killing them dogs, then it would be worth it."

"I guess we"ll have to take that as it comes," Mack said. "So for now, we'll draw up a contract, and you can stop by the office after work tonight and sign it.'"

"But your ad said you'd be closed by then." Dan said.

"Don't worry about that any. Someone will be there."

"Good enough," Dan agreed. "But I'd best be going now. My foreman is probably already in a bad mood."

They shook hands with Dan and he was off. Mack and Lisa reluctantly left the refuge and returned to their office. There would have been a lot more reluctance to return on their part, if their office was located in a town or city. Their's wasn't though. It was nestled in a small grove of trees which were part of a four hundred acre piece of land they jointly owned with Mack's father, Ben, his uncle, Roy, and their wives.

The office itself was a recently installed, new three bedroom, manufactured home. The kitchen inside was still a kitchen. Given the long hours often put in by the various partners in their detective agency, Refuge Rescuers, it was frequently used. The normal living area was the main office, with the entryway set aside as a greeting area for clients. The two smaller bedrooms were now primarily meeting rooms, and the third was the special office for one of the partners.

Sue Sartor was that partner. Inside her office she had and often used about every kind of electronic device available on the open market. She also had several that weren't. There wasn't much that she couldn't do with her equipment, so she was an intricate part of the agency.

All but one of the partners lived in their own homes located on the four hundred acres. Paul Danielson was a retired Minneapolis Police Detective. He worked as a detective in the Clayborne County Sheriff's department before joining Refuge Rescuers. He lived with his wife, Mary, on a small acreage a few miles from the office.

The remaining partners in the agency were Roy and Wanda Thomas. Roy was Mack's uncle. His father, Ben, and Ben's wife, Theresa, weren't directly part of the agency, but often gave their support.

One of the best things they did was prepare breakfast every morning for the staff of Refuge Rescuers, along with others who might be around and hungry when it was served.

Ben also raised forty acres of vegetables every summer. When he started farming, for years he sold his produce at the Minneapolis Farmer's Market. Now, since he didn't need the money any longer, he donated all the food he grew. It went to everything from food shelves to soup kitchens to local church festivals.

Ben's wife, Theresa worked in the fields with Ben, and raised chickens for eggs and meat. She also raised four pigs each year. Along with their normal food, they also ate a lot of produce that would have otherwise been wasted. Added to those chores, she managed the local community garden.

While Sue did the technical work, Mack and Lisa, both former deputy sheriffs, worked in the field. Roy and Wanda also worked as detectives in the field. Prior to that, they were ranchers and never did any kind of police work. Even so, they were very good at it. When necessary, or when he wanted to, Roy could talk himself out of nearly anything. He could also handle himself in a fight as well as any man.

Wanda was a woman you wouldn't want to mess with. If she needed to use a gun she was absolutely deadly. Especially with a rifle. She was also a person who rarely, if ever, showed the slightest sign of fear.

The agency also had a very valuable hidden asset. The sheriff of Clayborne County, Dale Magee. He was not only friends with every member of the agency, he firmly believed in what they were trying to accomplish.

They only had one employee. Julie Anderson, who also happened to be Lisa's younger sister. She worked as their receptionist and occasional secretary. She was young. A recent high school graduate just the previous spring, who was still totally undecided about what she wanted to do with the rest of her life.

Mack and Lisa, when they got back to the office, contacted all of those people who were away from the office, and arranged a meeting for late in the afternoon. Since both their meeting rooms were too small to accommodate all of them, they held the meeting at Ben and Theresa's. Their home was the original house on the four hundred acre plot of land, and had a dining room large enough to accommodate a lot of people. They always generously offered their huge dining room table for such meetings. And this time, like most times. they also provided refreshments and snacks.

"So," Roy, who always liked to start the conversation, be it at a meeting like this one or breakfast, said, "we have a new client."

"We do," Mack answered, and went on with an explanation that covered everything he knew about the client and the problem they were faced with.

"Dead dogs," Roy commented. "Now that's a strange one. It can all too often be a weird world out there, but dumping dead dogs by the dozens has got to be one of the strangest."

"It is," Mack agreed. "But more than that, those dogs were for some unknown reason killed before they were dumped. No one has the right to treat any animal like that. Especially dogs. There's no living animal, including other humans, who give back more for what they get, than what a dog does."

"I couldn't agree more," Detective Paul Danielson said. "And I agree that taking on this case is important. But where are you going to start? There doesn't seem to be any real clear path to follow."

Mack's already serious expression slipped into a frown. "No, there sure isn't. I do have a couple of ideas though."

"I never doubted that you would have." Paul smiled. "It pretty much seems as though you most always do."

"Maybe," Mack answered, "but I'm not at all sure how productive they'll be this time. But we have to start somewhere."

"Productive or not," Roy interrupted, "why don't you tell us what they are."

"They're pretty basic. To start with, I think you, Paul, should start checking out all dumps out of the county. At say, a hundred mile radius. See if they've had any dead dogs dumped. If so, get what you can out of the dump people about whoever did the dumping. We'll do the same with all the dumps in Clayborne County." Mack paused, took a deep breath, then went on with his ideas. "Lisa and I will be visiting the local dumps at quiting time, since it seems as though that's when the dogs are being dumped."

"When do you want to start working the dumps?" Paul asked.

"I think tonight, if Dan Tucker in fact makes it here to sign the contract. Lisa and I can check out the Main Street Dump. You can start canvassing the out of county dumps tomorrow."

Lisa spoke up then. "You are going to be on your own tonight, Mack. It's Thursday. Thursday is girl's night out. I missed the last two because you and I were working, so I'm going to go tonight. I have a feeling that this will be my last chance for a while. I'm pretty sure our newest case is going to keep us plenty busy."

"I can't argue with you about it," Mack said. "We have been working a lot lately, and you do deserve a night out with the girls." He smiled at Lisa. "Are all of you going to make it tonight?"

"We are. I even called dad to tell him Julie wouldn't be there for chores tonight." Lisa and Julie's father, Bob Anderson, was a dairy farmer. He milked just over a hundred cows twice each day, so when any of his children were home, they assisted with the milking.

"With Julie along tonight, I assume there won't be any drinking."

"You know, Mack, that there never is much on our nights out. We go mostly to just get away from the normal day to day, and talk about all the silly things we normally don't have time for. Tonight, Theresa's the designated (driver), so the rest of us might have a glass or two of wine. That, of course, does not include Julie."

"That sounds good. Just be careful. It seems like there's more of the miserables out there looking for trouble every day."

"I won't argue with you about that, Mack. But even so, I think you do worry a bit too much about us. We can take care of ourselves."

"I know you can, Lisa. But sometimes it seems like it even more dangerous for you guys, than for most woman."

"What makes you say that?"

"Now don't go calling me sexist for this, because what I'm saying is true. It's your looks. All of you are beautiful. Enough so that you could all be out there winning beauty contests. That does attract attention. Too much from the wrong people sometimes."

"I know. We'll be careful. We're going to that new place, out on the four lane. It's supposed to have really good food. They also have a separate bar with live music, tonight through the weekend. So we'll probably stick around for a while to see if the music is any good. So don't worry about us if we're a little later than usual."

"That sounds okay. But be damn careful about who you dance with."

"I will. You know my tolerance for jerks is zero."

"Good. And one last thing."

"What, Mack." Lisa looked at him to see if something was wrong. She hoped he wasn't getting jealous or something, because she would never give him the slightest reason for it.

He smiled at her. "Have a good time tonight. You've earned one."

CHAPTER 2

It was an uneventful night for Mack. He, and two elderly ladies, were the only last minute customers at the dump. So when he left there, he went to Ben's for supper. Something he and Roy usually did when there was a lady's night out.

For the lady's, the night started as good as they expected it would. Lisa and Julie were in the office when Dan Tucker came in and signed the contract for the job he wanted them to do. He was plenty early enough so he had no affect on their night out.

When they went, none of them wore anything special. Just clean and neat. What ever they had on, they couldn't help looking attractive. Because they were. Even in the simple blouse and jeans that Lisa, Wanda, and Sue wore. This night, Theresa and Julie stood out just a little more. They both wore basic cotton dresses that were always comfortable, even in a normal summer heat.

Theresa, even though she was old enough to be Julie's mother, was still a beautiful woman. And she had a special feature that made her stand out in any crowd. Her flaming red hair, still with so little gray in it, that red was the only color anyone ever noticed.

Julie carried the refreshing beauty of youth. It was only in the last year that her full figure of a woman had matured into the one she would be. And although she had slightly more of her father's features than Lisa had, she was every bit as beautiful.

Sues beauty tended more toward the dark and broody, and came across as a woman who any man would have to be a considerate, sharing type, to ever get close to her.

Wanda was simply all woman. One look at her was all that anyone needed to know it. Yet, at the same time, she was no one to be toyed with. And any man who tried would be in trouble. If they pushed too hard, one way or the other, she would push back hard enough for them to be sorry they ever did.

Lisa was, of all of them, the one who was simply outstanding. She still carried the look of youth, but her eyes carried a maturity that made one wonder who she really was, if they looked close enough. Her heart was bigger than most, and she thought little of money or things. Both of which she could have a lot of if she wanted them. Instead, she was more inclined to give away than she was to do for herself. She was kind to everyone deserving of kindness. As much as was humanly possible, she loved her husband. But when she was sixteen, she was kidnapped and raped multiple times. It was an experience which left a mark deep inside of her. A mark that said that there were certain men walking around in the world she lived in, who if they crossed her path, they were in trouble. She had spent years, working hard, training hard, to back up those feelings. If she was in a fight, she could beat most men. Often easily. And with those particular men, it was an activity she didn't mind participating in.

They all rode together when they went out that warm summer night. Theresa drove, and Wanda rode in the front seat with her. Lisa and Sue each sat next to a window in the back seat. Julie rode in the middle.

The new restaurant/bar they went to was already getting crowded when they arrived. Crowded enough so that if Theresa hadn't made reservations, they probably would have gone somewhere else.

The parking lot was also crowded, forcing them to park near the back of it. Their spot was in a place where the lighting would be poor when it got dark. Something, because of her experience, Lisa noted. The only even remotely positive thing she could see in it, was the fact they would all be leaving the place together.

Because the place was new, and the staff wasn't fully broken in, service was slow. They were forced to wait at a table in the bar before they were seated in the restaurant. Not too far away, seven construction workers from out of town were loudly making their presence known.

They, of course, immediately noticed the five women. After a few very rude and crude comments about their looks and various parts of their anatomies, two of the men walked up to their table.

"I think," one of the two said, his voice already slightly slurred from the several beers he'd already consumed, "that you fine looking babes need to join us at our table. I can guaranty you'll end up with everything you could ever want before the night is over."

They were the kind of men Lisa had zero tolerance for. And on this night, what they were doing was more than she was ready to take. She stood up and got into the man's face.

"There is nothing that I or any of the people sitting at this table could ever find even the slightest appealing about you or any of your friends. So please turn around and crawl back under whatever rock you were under."

"Well now, if you ain't a bitch, I don't know what one is. All I was trying to do is be friendly. And you being here without any men folks, it ain't hard to see what you're looking for."

"I asked you nicely to back off, asshole. So do it. Before I do it for you. I am not in the mood for your kind of crap."

"Now don't you talk tough, you silly little girl." He made the mistake of grabbing Lisa's arm and squeezing. "We both know that there's not a damn thing you can do to make me move if I don't want to."

That was enough for Lisa. Before he could even sense that something was about to happen, she slammed the palm of her free right hand on to his nose. She intentionally didn't break it, but blood rushed out, spilling over his mouth and dripping off his chin. She followed the blow by twisting his right arm behind him, lifting it too near the breaking point, and pushing him toward his table.

She spun around and faced the second man. "You leaving?" she asked him. "Or do you want to get hurt too?"

He tried glaring at her, sure he could intimidate her. He didn't. She glared back at him. He turned and walked back to his table. Wanda was standing next to Lisa by then. They watched for a moment, as all the men sympathized with their damaged friend. She shook her head, then turned to Liza.

"I think maybe we should consider going somewhere else for the night. Those creeps mean nothing but trouble."

"I know," Lisa agreed. "And I guess I shouldn't have been quite so hard on the jerk. But I get so damn tired of men like that. Why the hell can't they leave us alone. I would rather be dead than do with them what they want to do to me. What they want to do to every one of us, actually."

"You didn't do anything wrong," Wanda told her. "If I would have been sitting where you were, I would have done the same thing you did. But I think it would be a good idea to leave now. It won't be a good thing to have to deal with them out in that dark parking lot later."

"I've got a better idea," Lisa smiled now. "We've never done this before, but I think it's time we did. Those assholes over at that table need a lesson if they try to do anything with us later. So let's give them one."

About fifteen minutes later, they were taken to their table in the dining area. They saw no sign of the seven men while they ate. The meal proved to be mediocre, so they found themselves wishing they'd gone somewhere else for that reason alone.

When they finished eating, they decided they might as well check out the band and music that was just starting up. Neither was any better than the food. Lisa made a phone call, and they waited for a while near the bar. Lisa, Wanda, and Sue had a glass of wine while they did. Theresa and Julie each had a coke.

All the time they were there, the seven, now nine, construction workers watched them closely. When it came time to leave, it didn't surprise Lisa or Wanda at all to see all nine of the men watching them leave their table and follow them out. The men waited until they were near Wanda's car before they made their move.

A different man than the first bothersome two spoke up this time. "What you done to our friend was way out of line, you know." He was grinning while he talked. "So now, everyone of you is going to have to say you're sorry."

"Be a cold day in hell before that will ever happen," Wanda told him. "The truth is, you boys are the ones who will be saying I'm sorry."

"Now you are talking stupid. You will be saying you are sorry. And you will be doing it by getting rid of those clothes you're wearing. Starting right now."

He tired to grab Wanda's blouse so he could rip it open. All he got was a broken wrist when Wanda grabbed his hand and gave it the proper twist. At the same time, Lisa took out the man closest to her with a well aimed kick to the groin.

And that's when the construction workers learned their lesson about how to properly treat women. Mack, Roy, Ben, and sheriff Dale Magee suddenly appeared. They'd been waiting in Dale's car, just out of sight.

"You can all lay face down now," Dale told them. "You are under arrest."

The men looked at each other, then lunged at what they now considered their enemy. It was a very foolish mistake. In less than two minutes they were all on the ground. Only some of them were bleeding, but all of them were soundly beaten.

Now it was time for Dale to make a call, and in a short time all nine men were checked by medics and then taken to jail. In the morning they were given the choice between giving up their jobs and going back to wherever it was they came from, or facing a judge in court. All nine of the men were well on their way to their far away home by late afternoon.

When Mack, Lisa, and the rest of the family talked about it over breakfast, they all agreed that Lisa didn't have to feel guilty for not putting up with the construction workers.

Ben summed it up for all of them when he said, "There are times when you just have to put a stop to the bullshit."

CHAPTER 3

Mack and Lisa decided to work together as they went to talk to the people at the three other dumps. At the first one they went to, the foreman was a rather plump lady. She had a tangled head of brown hair, heavily mixed with gray. She was once a more than pretty woman, but now considered taking care of herself a waste of time. She had no need to impress anyone, and didn't much care for men. Her attitude about most things came from her husband. He was a lecher and a drunk, who now at her insistence, slept in what was once their only child's bedroom. The same single bed the child slept in was still there.

She laughed when Mack explained to her why they were there. "Dead dogs? You want to know if we've had dead dogs dumped here. About the only thing we haven't had dumped here is a human body. Not yet anyway. At least, not that I know about it."

"We're not talking about an occasional dog," Mack again explained. "We'd like to know it lately there's been a much larger number of dogs dumped recently. Like two or more at a time."

"Only once, so far as I know. One of the guys, Chester, he said there was a bag of about three of them. Two German Shepards and a Golden Retriever I think."

"What did you do with them?"

"Same thing we do with everything else around here. Covered them up so they wouldn't smell too much. People around here always bitch if something gets too smelly."

"You didn't report it to animal control?"

"What for. The dogs were dead. Like I said, we covered them up. Same like we do with everything. Like we did with that bag of dead cats that was dumped the other day. Must have been thirty in that garbage bag. You can just never know what it is that people might throw away."

"No, I guess you don't. Would it be okay if we talk to your guys about the dogs? On the chance they might have seen dogs they didn't tell you about?"

"If you can get their attention, go ahead. Just don't take too long with them. Things get difficult if we get behind on the stuff coming in. Sometimes when that happens, we have to work overtime. Paying overtime always pisses the owners off. Raises hell with their billions."

Mack and Lisa drove out into the dump. They parked well away from the areas where various garbage moving machines were working. They left the pickup and walked over to where they were working. As soon as they were in a spot where a man driving a D9 could see them, Mack tried to flag him down. The driver totally ignored them. The same thing happened again with that driver on Mack's second try. When he tried with a different driver, the reaction didn't change.

"I think," Liza told him, "I might have better luck."

"Really now. Why would you?"

"That, Mack, is a silly question, and you know it." She stood close, facing him. She unbuttoned the two top closed buttons on her blouse. She still hadn't revealed anything, but the open buttons hinted she might have. "That's why," she said, giving Mack a wide grin.

He returned it and said, "Go ahead, get us someone we can get some answers from."

When she waved her arms at the first driver to look at her, he pulled up close to her and shut his rig down. "What can I do for you?" he asked, staring at her neck, wishing she'd opened a few more buttons.

"Just answer a few questions," she said. "About some dead dogs."

"You've got to be kidding me. I stop working, which I never should do, to help out a pretty lady and she wants to know about dead dogs. What the hell is this old world coming too?"

"To no good, I think," Lisa said. "That's why I need to know if you've seen more dogs than usual dumped here lately?"

"I have, yes. So have all the guys. But why does that concern such a pretty lady as you?"

"It's our job. We don't know why the dogs are being dumped. We are trying to find out why. Right now, we are checking out the places where they might have been dumped. Did you or any of the other guys see who did any of the dumping?"

"I didn't. Mostly, they were dumped at the end of the day, when only the foreman was here. And she wouldn't have a way of knowing. She has to stay in her shack, so she can collect the money. She couldn't watch what they dumped."

"Okay, thanks. I appreciate your help."

"You are welcome," he said, this time letting his eyes drift down some. "And if there's ever anything else I can do for you, let me know." He gave her a big smile, got on his rig, fired it up and went back to work.

Mack, who was standing back to let Lisa do the talking, moved closer. "Well, did you learn anything?"

"There have been more dogs. So far as he knows, they were dumped at the end of the day, the same as the other dump."

"Did you ask him about the cats?"

"Sorry, no. He couldn't take too much time with me. The bosses don't like it when they stop for anything. I'll ask the next one."

"Okay. I'm going to let you do the talking for the rest of these dump visits. But I'm going to stay with you. It'll cut the chances of any trouble."

"That's fine by me. I like your company anyway."

When they left the dump, they'd learned that all of the moving equipment operators had seen dead dogs. Usually in groups of three to five. The exceptions were two bags of ten or more of small dogs. And for the rest of the men she talked to, she remembered to ask about the cats. It turned out that there were several bags of them. Usually containing ten to fifteen cats in each one.

"I have to believe that the reason for the dead cats is related to the dead dogs," Mack said.

"I agree. They are part of the mystery. The more we learn about this, the less sense it makes. Who the hell is it, do you think, that's killing all those animals. It's so damn cruel. It just doesn't make any sense."

"I know, Lisa. Killing like this never does. And when it's on this scale, it double doesn't make sense."

The man running the next dump was anything but pleased to see them. He was younger than the first two, and hesitant about answering their questions. It took a lengthy explanation from Mack to get anything out of the man. Even then, his first answers were complaints about his own life.

"It's like this," he said. "No matter what you tell me, I can't be sure what your real reasons for being here are. And I don't have the time to figure it out. I've got enough problems as it is. It's all I can do to run this place. It's not even mine. It's my old man's. The only reason I'm here is because he had a heart attack. I'm only supposed to be temporarily filling in until he gets better. Something I don't think is going to happen. That means I'll be stuck here. And you want me to worry about some dead dogs."

"I'm not asking you to worry about them," Mack argued. "I'm only asking if there have been more dogs dumped here lately than normal."

"I haven't been here long enough to know for sure what is or isn't normal. If anything going on in a dump can be called normal. But, yes, I think I heard some complaining about some extra dogs being dumped. I don't know if it matters to you, but cats too. Lots of cats, I think. Bags full."

"That's what we are here to find out," Lisa told him. She spoke softly, hoping to sooth his obviously jangled nerves some. "Will it be okay if we talk to your employees, and ask them about the dead dogs and cats. We are also trying to find out who's been dumping them. What they're doing is illegal."

"I guess, just so long as you don't take up too much of their time. The one thing I know about this place. It can be easy to fall behind on the work."

Lisa managed to get the attention of all the operators, one at a time. They were all helpful, but none of them could even guess who it was that did the dumping. The only hitch came after she finished with the last operator. He was in his mid twenties, and his once near perfect athletic body was just beginning to show signs of going to seed. Since his high school football and baseball ended, he'd neglected most physical training. Operating the machine he did, often was tiring and did give him some exercise, but not enough to keep him in the shape he thought he was in. He also considered himself to be handsome, and the kind of man any woman would love to be around. So, naturally he couldn't let a woman like Lisa just walk away.

"Now," he said to her, "before you go, since I answered all your questions, how about you answer one for me?"

"If it's a proper question, I'd be glad to."

"What's your phone number?"

"Sorry." She smiled. "That's not a proper question. I'm married and not in the least bit interested. The man I'm with is my husband. Thank you again for your help. Have a good day."

"That scar faced jerk is your husband. He don't look like much of a man to me. I bet he don't come close to keeping you happy. Not like I could anyway."

Lisa sighed, wondering why men like him were always so childish and stupid. For her, the scars on Mack's face said a lot about him. He got those scars from a shotgun blast. He had given her a ride home on a miserable winter night, when she was still a kid. He was shot as he stopped in his own driveway when he got back home. She always felt like she was the cause. He never even slightly indicated that he felt that way. So for her, rather than being something ugly, the scars made him more handsome, more real, and more of a man than anyone she'd ever known. So much better than the childman in front of her. Enough that she was almost surprised that they could breath the same air. Without bothering to answer him, she turned and walked away.

"Something wrong?" Mack asked when he saw the look on her face.

"Same old, same old," she answered. "I got what I could from them. But none of them knows who's been doing the dumping. Anyway, let's get the hell out of here."

The football player watched them leave. As he did, he realized that he would never get anywhere close to Lisa. No matter what he did. Not after he saw the look she gave him.

CHAPTER 4

The visit to the last dump in the county yielded the same results as the others. There was still a couple of hours left in the afternoon when they finished up, so they went back to the office. They sat down with Sue, and put what information they had in the computer, so Sue could organize it in a way to better analyze it as more data came in.

When that task was complete, she asked Mack, "what are your plans for the rest of the afternoon?"

"None, until it's time to watch the late dumping at the Main Street Dump. Is there something you need me to do?"

"Not need exactly. But if you have time, it would be a big help if you could run into the bank for me. Between yesterday and today, it seems as though most of our clients decided to pay us. I'll be late getting done tonight, so you could save me a late trip to the bank."

"No problem. I'll go for you. By the time I do that, and stop and fill up the truck, I can check out the dump. They'll be close enough to closing by then. All of the equipment operators will be gone by then anyway."

"That's right. Their eight hour shift is shorter than the dumps hours of operation. It's no wonder people get away with so much illegal dumping."

"If you don't mind, Mack," Lisa said, "I think I'll quit on you for the day. I'd like to spend a little time with the horses. Before they forget who I am."

"Go ahead. It'll be good for you too. We'll think about supper when I get home."

"I've got a better idea. Pick up a large garbage pizza when you're done. Save both of us cooking tonight."

"Will do." Mack looked at Sue. "You're working late too. How about I give you a call on my way home. You can share the pizza with us."

"I'd love to."

Mack was glad he had extra time when he got to the bank. They were missing a teller and there was a line. He made it to the dump with plenty of time anyway. But the time he spent there was fruitless. There was no suspicious dumping. So he headed to the truck stop to fill up. He planned to order the pizza when he got there, so it would be ready when he finished filling the truck and washing the windows.

He made the call for the pizza, and had just started filling his gas tank when Roy and Wanda pulled up to the gas pumps right behind him. Before he could acknowledge the fact they were there, a large, black SUV stopped at the front entry. It was a no parking zone. Three men got out, but the driver stayed in the vehicle. Mack didn't like what he was seeing.

He turned toward Roy, who was also watching the men. Roy then looked at Mack. They nodded at each other as a way of agreeing that something bad could very well be happening. Something that shouldn't be. Something that was a serious problem.

The inside of the building was filled with all kinds of people. Way too many for them to go in and do anything to stop what was going on. If, in fact, something wrong was going on. Before they could decide what to do, a gunshot rang out, quickly followed by a second one. One at a time, the three armed men rushed out. The leader of them held a little girl in his arms. He seemed to be using her as a shield.

Mack, Roy, and Wanda were all armed, but Mack and Roy were hesitant to shoot. Wanda wasn't. Two well placed shots took down two of the men. But not even Wanda, as good a shot as she was, would trust a pistol shot against the third man. Not with that little girl in his arms. He managed to get in the car he came in.

The man fired at Wanda, and drove away.. The bullet he fired hit a metal pole next to her. That should have left her safe, but fragments of the bullet hit her. They wounded her in three places in her side. She instantly went down.

Roy rushed to her side while Mack called 911. The sirens started a minute later. A Kingsburg cop was patrolling the closest, so he was first to arrive. More city cops and several sheriff's deputies followed. It was mostly disorganized grab ass until the chief of police and Sheriff Dale Magee arrived.

Because he was the most experienced cop there, Dale took charge. The first thing he did was check on Wanda. "How bad?" he asked Roy.

"'I'm not sure. But I'll feel a damn sight better when the ambulance gets here."

He no more than said that, then the ambulance's siren filled he air, and in a moment or two, was there. They immediately took over Wanda's care. Roy had gotten her bleeding under control. They got it stopped.

The lead man working on her turned to Roy and said, "It looks worse than what it is. You did good controlling the bleeding. It would have been a lot worse if you hadn't."

With that, they loaded her on the stretcher, and in a couple of minutes their siren was screaming as they headed to the hospital. Roy was right behind them. A city cop followed Roy, its siren wailing too. They were doing their best to keep him safe from other traffic on the short ride there.

Dale checked out the men laying on the concrete in front of the truck stop. Both were dead. Wanda made sure that both shots she fired were deadly. She knew how dangerous return fire could be. If it hadn't have been for the little girl, the third man would have been dead too.

Both of the cashiers inside were also dead. Shot in the head at close range. They were both females. Both in their midtwenties, and both people who would have had a lot of life in front of them, had they been given the chance.

Mack called Lisa as soon as the ambulance came for Wanda, then waited for Dale. When he joined Mack, the look on his face told him that things had gone very wrong. Mack didn't say anything until after Dale did.

"Both of the cashiers inside are dead. So damn young. Two beautiful young women. Killed for something I'll never understand."

"It's wrong, that's for damn sure," Mack said. "But at least Wanda took two of them out. She'd gotten the third one too, if he hadn't have been holding that kid."

"Yeah, the kid. If you don't mind, Mack, I'd like to have you hang around for a while. But now, I've got to find the mother of the kid. She needs to know what happened."

"She does. And you never know, there could be some kind of a connection, between the kid being taken and what went down."

"Not likely, but it is possible."

It was somewhat over an hour before Dale returned. He was shaking his head when he did. He looked at Mack, then shook his head even harder. "You were right, Mack, when you said there might be some kind of connection between what went down and the kid. The bastards did rob the place, but that wasn't the main reason for them being here tonight. The man who carried the kid out was her father. The mother was one of the dead cashiers. She was divorcing her husband, and asking the court for full custody of the child. The kid was here because she couldn't get a babysitter tonight."

"You mean the asshole murdered her because of that? That's about as low as it gets."

"It is. The one good thing about it, we now have a name. So it shouldn't be too difficult to track him down. He'll be one man I will be more than happy to lock up."

"That will be a good day, Dale. The only thing better would be if he seriously resists arrest."

"Come on, Mack, you don't really prefer that he's killed, do you?"

"Actually, I would. There are some life forms that are useless. And I think they are pretty much all human."

"You don't believe then, that all human life is sacred?"

"I sure as hell don't. That statement is one of the biggest pieces of bullshit ever spoken."

Dale almost laughed. "You know, Mack," he said, "sometimes you are more right than even you know. The man who did the killing was Savage Strange. A fitting name for such a stupid, useless creature. Savage Strange. That ain't even the half of it."

"The strangest part of it all, Dale, is the fact that we humans still exist, given how often we've produced creatures like him. It's too bad Roy and I couldn't stop him. But how the hell could we go in there and create a situation that could have too easily turned into a gunfight. It was just too damn crowded."

"You did the right thing, Mack. It's not likely you could have stopped the killing inside. And if you'd gone in, a lot more people could have been hurt or killed."

"I know. But I think I'll give Lisa another call, then go see how Wanda's doing."

Mack made the call. When Lisa answered, she said that she, Sue, and Ben and Theresa were already at the hospital. They would see him when he got there.

Mack left Dale then, hoping against hope that Wanda would be okay. He loved her as much as he could have loved a sister, if he would ever have had one. He couldn't imagine a life without her in it.

CHAPTER 5

Dale Magee's wife, Kathy, waited for him on the couch. She was in the living room of their rather large house. A house she wanted, but that he never cared much about one way or the other. Money and things were not what he wanted in life.

When they met, she was about everything he wanted. He fell in love with her right away. She with him soon after. Those early days with him were filled with memories, running from good too great. Like many young couples, it was a struggle. Money was always tight, and his job as a new sheriff in Clayborne County took a lot more from him than just his time.

But he'd always done his best, and as much as he possibly could, he always put her first. He still put her first, even though she didn't expect him to.

She was a singer. She had been all her life. Once she was an adult, she started singing professionally. Her career blossomed quickly, and now she was rich and famous. She loved that part of her life. The problem was, Dale never complained about any aspect of it, but there was no way he could ever be part of it.

They still loved each other, she knew, so she waited for him. When he did get home, he was surprised she wasn't in bed. They had long ago agreed that she didn't have to wait up for him on the nights his job made him as late as he was on this night.

"I love it that you're awake," he said. "But why are you?"

She didn't answer. She took his hand and led him to their bedroom. She dropped the robe she was wearing on the floor. As she moved to the bed, her eyes told him to get undressed and join her.

As soon as he was next to her, she did what she needed to do to make him ready, then pulled him over her. She loved him then, with a kind of urgency that she'd never done before. Neither one of them lasted very long. When he moved off her, she finally spoke her first word that night.

She started with, "We have to talk now."

"Okay," he agreed. "You talk, I'll listen." His stomach was suddenly in tight knots. Her words, the tone of her voice, told him something was wrong. Real wrong.

"As you know, I'm going on tour again. This will be the longest one ever. About a full year."

"Do you want me to go with you. I will, if that's what you want."

"No. We both know that the one time you did, you were miserable the whole time. No, Dale, I don't want you to do anything like that."

"I can tell, Kathy, that there's something you want. What is it?"

"A divorce."

Dale jolted up in the bed. He couldn't believe what she'd just said. "You can't be serious. Why. What did I do?"

"You didn't do anything wrong, Dale. What's wrong is life, and how it changes things. Time is a killer too. Life and time has changed who and what we are. Where we live. It's two different worlds that we live in. You with your job. Me with mine. They have nothing to do with each other. We barely talk to each other anymore."

"I'll try to do better. Anything. If it's my job that bothers you, I'll quit."

"I wish it was that simple. I won't quit, and that's the problem. What kind of life is it when I'm gone more than I am home. We just don't have a real marriage any longer. We are often more like strangers. And this time, it's going to be a year."

"I know, Kathy. But we could still see each other. You could sometimes fly home, or I could fly to wherever you are." His voice was pleading now.

"We could do that. There's a problem though. If we do something like that, I'll always be so exhausted that often you'll be lucky to get so much as a smile out of me."

Dale was at a loss for words. She obviously was serious. She wanted a divorce. That led him to the dreaded conclusion. He asked her the question that was always an accusation. "Is there someone else? Is that what's wrong."

She cried then. Between sobs, she answered. "No, Dale, there's no one else. Not now. It's not that I haven't been tempted. I have, but I've always loved you too much to let anything happen. A year on tour though, anything could happen. I don't want to be a cheating wife, and with what else that is wrong between us, I think it's best we split while we still care about each other."

"Isn't there any way I can talk you out of this. That I can stop this."

She wiped her eyes with a corner of the bed sheet. "No, there really isn't. I've known for a long time that we were drifting too far apart to be able to continue living this way.

"Earlier tonight," he said, tears now running down his face, "I thought that the horror I was dealing with then, was the worse thing I'd have to deal with for a long time. I see now that I was wrong. I know, Kathy, that you think what you are doing is the right thing. It isn't, and never will be. You can have your divorce. But you have to know, you just broke my heart."

She didn't answer. She cried again as she rolled over on her side, her back to him. He laid down next to her, wrapping his arms around her and pulling her close.

The lay quietly until her shaking stopped. She turned to face him. She kissed him. He returned it. Many more followed. She opened her legs and he moved over her. They joined together and loved each other for a long time.

When they parted, he kissed her one more time, then left the bed. He dressed, took a small suitcase from a closet, and started to pack his clothes. She watched him for a while, surprised at his actions.

"Are you planning to leave now?" she asked. "You don't have to do that already. I'll be gone in two days. You'll have a year then to leave this house."

"No, Kathy. I can't stay here at all. I'm just going to take some clothes for now. Enough for those two days. Then I'll get the rest of my stuff out of here. This house is yours. It always has been."

"But you can still stay for the next two days. We can wait until I leave for my tour before we finally split."

"I don't think so." He finished with the suitcase and closed it. "This is the last time you and I will ever have any kind of close contact with each other. Whatever you do from now, until the end of your life, it will be without me in it."

"It sounds like you hate me, Dale." She choked back a sob. "Do you?"

"No, I don't hate you. I hope you have a happy life ahead of you. But I haven't stopped loving you, the way you have me. So I can't look at you anymore. As you said, our life together is over. So it's over."

"Just like that. You are going to walk away tonight, when you don't really have too. We could still have something for our last two days together."

"The years we had were, for me, good ones. Perfect, no. But nothing's perfect. Those years are gone now, and I will forever be trying to wipe them all from my memory. As far as I'm concerned, a huge part of my life is gone now. And nothing can ever bring it back."

"I've hurt you that bad?"

"Hell, that's just a start. You'll never know, never feel the hurt you've dumped on me tonight."

Dale picked up his suitcase and without another word, walked away. The last thing he heard was Kathy. Just one word. "No."

CHAPTER 6

Roy stopped at Ben and Theresa's in the morning. He had no interest in eating breakfast. Food was the last thing he wanted. His main concern was Wanda, and he was anxious to get to the hospital to see her. The only other thing on his mind was Savage Strange. He was the reason Wanda was in the hospital, so he wanted to know more about the man. He asked Mack for a favor while he was there.

"Will you, Mack," Roy asked, "get with Sue today? Find out what you can about that Strange guy."

"I can do that. But do you think we really need to? The law will likely arrest him. Could be as soon as today."

"It could be as soon as never too. So I'd really appreciate if if you could get with Sue."

"Okay, Roy. I will."

Roy left and the rest of them ate breakfast. When it was done, Ben and Theresa did the cleanup. Lisa went out and did some of Theresa's chores. She especially enjoyed letting the chickens out of their coop. Their enthusiasm for the outdoors every morning was as about life affirming as anything could get. Watching them, brought joy to the hearts of most people who had that privilege.

There was no joy, however, to be found in researching Savage Strange. From the time he was a kid, he'd been in trouble. All of it resulting from a vicious temper. A temper that was used on smaller, weaker people, and even innocent animals.

He was arrested several times for abusing his younger sister and his mother. Still, when he had control of his temper, he could be charming. He had the kind of looks that could, when he made the effort, charm a woman. It was what he used to court and convince his now dead wife to marry him.

All in all, his record showed that he was the kind of person whose best contribution he could have made to society as a whole, would to have never been born. But he was, and now he had committed murder and kidnapped his own daughter. A daughter he didn't want. Not before she was born. Not after. He took her to hurt his wife. Who was now dead and could no longer be hurt.

His financial history wasn't any different than anything else about him. Suspicious described it best. He rarely held down a job. When he did they were short lived. Deposits in his bank account were few and far between. But when they were made, they were relatively large. Often though, the money would quickly disappear. When he made withdrawals from his account, they were most often from ATM machines. Most of the time located in casinos. He tended to like the one near Mille Lacs Lake the best.

Because she could easily do it, and because he so surely deserved it, Sue made it all disappear. She also closed out all of his credit cards. There was a chance he could get them reinstated, but it would be difficult.

Sue and Mack noted his address, but were sure that by then the police were already there, so they didn't check into it any further. The main thing they knew when they shut down the files on him, was what they already suspected. He was a useless, miserable excuse for a human. He easily represented nearly everything the human race needed to rid itself of.

Mack then asked Sue, "Do you want to ride with Lisa and I to the hospital?"

"Thanks for the offer," she said, "but I think I'll drive. I've got a lot to to do today, so I'll probably be leaving there before you guys do."

"That's okay. But you know, on days like today, no one will get upset if you get a little behind."

"No one else will, Mack." She smiled. "But I will. The stuff I'm working on now, can be a bitch to catch up with if I get behind. So it's best if I don't. I'm pretty sure Wanda will understand that."

"We all will. We'll see you when you get there then."

Ben and Theresa had already left for the hospital, so Mack found Lisa waiting for him at home. She was ready to go, so they left right away. It was a quiet ride. They knew that Wanda wasn't hurt as bad as they initially feared. Their concern for her weighed heavily on their minds anyway.

Wanda's room was private, but too small for more than three or four people at a time. Since a lot of her family was there, along with Roy's family and the rest of the Refuge Rescuers staff, there was a wait to see her.

Dale was in the room when they got there, but he came out soon after they did. He only stopped for a few moments to say hello to Ben, Theresa, Mack, and Lisa, then left.

When he was gone, Lisa turned to Mack, the look of confusion on her face. "What do you think is wrong with Dale?" she asked. "I've never seen that look on his face before. It was as if someone died. Or something horrible happened."

"I noticed," Mack answered her. "I don't have the slightest idea what it is, but there damn sure is something wrong."

"Maybe Wanda will know. She talked to him longer than we did. She's better at finding out about things like that than we are. Maybe she'll have some answers."

Sue came into the waiting room then. Mack intercepted her and warned her about the wait.

"I think I'll head back to the office then. But not before you tell me about Dale. You guys did get to see him?"

"Only for a minute or two."

"Did you see the look he had? What do you think is wrong?"

"I wish I knew," Mack said. "Whatever it is going on with him, it looks real serious."

"It does that. Please let me know if you find out what it is."

"We'll do that, Sue."

It was another twenty minutes before they got to see Wanda. She was sitting up in the bed, her face remarkably free of the usual tubes and tape. Roy was next to her, sitting on a stool that was taller than the normal chair. He was holding her hand. Paul Danielson was the fourth person in the room.

"I know it's crowded," he said, "but I knew you two were coming in next. I wanted to talk to you for a couple of minutes."

"That was a good idea. I'm real curious as to how you are doing with the dog and cat thing."

"Let's meet for lunch. We can go over that then." Shaking his head, Paul shrugged his shoulders. "It's Dale I wanted to talk to you about."

"Do you know what's going on with him?" Lisa asked. "When we saw him, he looked awful upset about something."

"That he is."

Wanda spoke up then. "It took some to get him to talk about it. When he finally did, he was almost incoherent. He kept choking up, so he didn't say much. But the gist of it is, Kathy asked for a divorce."

"Why the hell would she do that?" Lisa said. *Too Dale!* He would never do any of the things people do to cause a divorce. He is such a good, kind, generous man. And he's always treated her like she's a princess, or a queen even."

"I tried to get him to talk about it, but he wasn't able. He's pretty broken up over it. It's going to be hard for him to deal with. If they'd let me get the hell out of this hospital, I'd go find him. Even if he won't talk, I could at least hold his hand for a while."

"I can do that," Lisa said. She looked at Mack. "Will that be okay?"

"I'll take you home, so you can go in your own truck."

They made their goodbye with Wanda, Roy, and Paul. When they were gone, Paul said. "Now that's as trusting as it gets."

Wanda looked at Roy and winked. "Trusting each other, Paul, is what we do. None of us are perfect, but none of us would ever intentionally do anything to hurt each other. What Lisa will do for Dale will be okay. And it won't make Mack hurt at all. Not at all."

Mack knew, as he watched Lisa drive away, that what Wanda said was true. He didn't have to hear her say it to know. Lisa would comfort Dale. She truly would hold his hand. Maybe hold him. Nothing else. Her bond with him was too strong for anything else.

Around noon, he met Paul for lunch. Dale was on their minds, along with Wanda. Lisa was there too. But she was more of a concern for Paul than Mack, who decided right away to steer the conversation toward the dead animal case.

"Have you learned much, Paul?" he asked right away. "About the dead animal dumping?"

"Not enough, I'm afraid. I only made it to four dumps yesterday. All of them took longer than what they should have. It's really damn hard to get the attention of those guys working those dumps. And when I did, none of them would give me much of their time."

"If your experience was much like mine, they didn't tell you all that much either."

"No, they didn't. All of them, everyone in all four dumps, saw more dead dogs and cats than normal. A few had the misfortune of seeing a lot of dead cats and dogs."

"Anyone one at all witness anyone dumping them?"

"No. It was the same problem you've had. End of day dumping, when only the lead person was still there. And of course, they were always too busy to notice."

"Do you think it will be worth watching any of the dumps, to see if we can catch anyone dumping?"

"It might, Mack. But since we are limited to how much we can do, I think I can contribute more by visiting dumps. I think I should continue to check them farther away each time. It would be good to know how far this has gone. It's already far bigger a problem than I thought it would or could be."

"I have to agree with you, Paul. We need to get a better picture on the size of this problem. We've reached the point now, that I no longer care how big it is, I want answers. I also believe that whatever is going on, it is something that needs to be stopped."

"I can't argue that. Not at all. All that killing. Damnit, I love dogs. I can't say I feel all that positive about cats. But my wife loves them. She owns two of them. I haven't told her yet, what I'm working on. I know she's going to be real upset when I do."

"If this gets into the media, it will upset a lot of people. A hell of a lot more than what we will want to deal with."

"You've got that right, Mack. Time comes, if it gets out we are involved in this case, we'll be buried in animal lovers. Not to mention, ordinary people who happen to own a dog or cat."

"When the time comes, we'll have to try to push them off on the official law enforcement. They won't like it much, because they are often short handed too. But they are still better equipped to deal with the public than we are."

"Being short handed something we both remember. And speaking of that, how is the sheriff's department doing now? Is

Dale going to be able to go after that Savage Strange guy. I can't see the Kingsburg police being able to do much. Even if they had enough cops, none of them are trained well enough to deal with men like him. Especially with a kid involved."

"I guess we'll have to wait and see."

"That we will, Mack. I'm going to take the rest of the day off. I'll be doing a lot of driving the next few days, so they'll be long ones. I want to spend a little time with my wife, before I have to neglect her again."

Paul caught Mack's eye then, and Mack knew he was real curious about Lisa. And how Mack felt about what she might be doing with Dale. He didn't want to discuss it with Paul. But he did.

"What Lisa is doing now is trying to help a friend get through a crisis," he explained without being asked. "I totally trust her, Paul. As much as that, I trust Dale. Upset as he is right now, he's the most standup guy I've ever known. It wouldn't matter if Lisa invited him to do more that they should, it's highly unlikely he would. So you can stop wondering. What's going on is no more than a simple act of kindness."

Paul blushed a little, embarrassed for pushing Mack to give him the answer he did. "I'm sorry, Mack. I really shouldn't think the way I do. I was too long in the cities. I saw too much. Most of the cops I worked with were damn good people. But some acted as if it was their mission to not only screw up their lives, but too many others too."

"Don't worry about it. We live in that kind of a world now. Trust is something hard to come by. So is friendship. That means if my wife can comfort the man who's been my best friend for a long time when he needs it. So be it. It's all good. It's all innocent. But even if it wasn't, sometimes I'm not so sure what would be right."

They were done. Mack paid for the lunch and they left. When he got to his truck, started it and put on his seat belt, his phone rang. It was Lisa.

CHAPTER 7

The cabin was small, dark, and dirty from lack of use the past five years. It was a lousy place to be, but when a person needed to hide out, there weren't that many places to go. So a deserted cabin, deep in the north woods, would have to be sufficient for now. Savage Strange wouldn't even have this, if hadn't belonged to an uncle of his. His mother's brother owned it until he died. Since his wife was already dead and they didn't have children, no one picked up the small mortgage on it. It went to the bank, and sat there idle ever since.

It still could be a decent place to stay, had he brought enough food and water along. And maybe a few cleaning supplies and something for the bed. But all he had was a few things he hastily grabbed from his home after the shooting at the truck stop. He knew right away, he would have to take a chance and go do some shopping.

He took his constantly whimpering three year old daughter out to the car with him, and left to find the nearest discount store. He was hoping to find a Walmart, because he thought they were the cheapest. But he would accept anything, under the current circumstances.

When Savage found one, he nearly filled his cart with basic household supplies, which he paid for with cash from the truck stop robbery. Along with everything else, he remembered bedding for the bed he planned to sleep on. He figured the kid could sleep on the couch. He could cover her with jackets or coats or something.

Among the things he forgot were clothes and diapers for his daughter. It never occurred to him that she might not be able to handle long periods away from the bathroom. He also couldn't see a reason to change her clothes. The other two things he forgot were a can opener for the large assortment of canned food he bought, and matches for the gas cook stove that needed to be hand lit. It was too old for an automatic burner lighting system.

On the way back to the cabin, while still on the highway, he drove by the Grand Casino Mille Laces. He managed to make it a mile up the highway before the fever hit him. There was no way he could not stop. Not when he was sure he would win. He wouldn't be there too long. Just a few hands of Black Jack.

Savage gave his daughter a couple of candy bars, a can of soda, and left her in the locked car. He was wrong about winning, but he was right about not being in the casino long. He lost all the cash he had left from the truck stop robbery in the first three hands he played.

He searched around then, for an ATM. It pleased him when he found one not far from the table he was playing. He first tried to withdraw money from his checking account. He was rejected. He knew he had money in it, so he tried again, three more times. No luck. He tried one of his credit cards. Again, he was rejected. He was forced to give up and leave the casino after all of his credit cards rejected his attempts to withdraw money. They should have been good. He was an extremely angry man. He was sure that the law must have gotten into them and closed them. So now he was in trouble. He needed money and didn't have any. What to do?

He didn't hesitate at the next truck stop. He drove right in. He stopped in front of the building. He took his automatic from the glove box and pushed it in his belt. He looked at his daughter, wondering what to do with her. He then decided to take her with him. He thought she might be good cover.

Holding her hand, he walked her inside. She was cute. Cute always attracts the right kind of attention. They went straight to one of the cashiers. She jumped back in fright when he pointed his gun at her.

"Put your money in a bag and I won't hurt you," he told her.

She did as Savage asked and gave him the bag. He turned around and started to walk out of the place. With his back to her, she screamed. He spun around and shot her. She fell, and the man next to him tried to grab him. He shot the man, then picked up his daughter. He knew she made a good shield. At least she did when it was a cop who would do the shooting. They had too much respect for the kid's life to ever chance a shot while he was holding her.

The exception would have been a police sniper, who was an expert with a rifle. The expert would also need to be stationed in a place with a clear shot at Savage's head. Unfortunately, none of them were stationed in the truck stop.

There was, however, a slightly overweight, middle aged male who belonged to a paramilitary group. He was carrying a forty-five caliber revolver. He considered himself to be a marksman with his powerful handgun, even though he'd never scored higher than low average at the target range. He stood back in the crowd of people. He did not have a good, clear shot at Savage

It didn't matter to him though. He'd fired enough bullets with his buddies from his military group, to now consider himself a warrior's warrior. And this was his chance to prove it.

Like any good member of the NRA would do, he took careful aim at Savage Strange and pulled the trigger. As he did, Savage's daughter pulled away from him a few inches. The two of them were standing sideways from the NRA warrior, when the bullet missed him. It didn't miss his daughter. It hit her in her head.

Blood, bone, and tissue splattered the crowd and Savage. He dropped her and ran for the stores exit. In the confusion from the gunshot, Savage managed to make it to the exit and escape the store. The warrior reached it at the same time.

Savage shot him in the hand that held the forty-five, and forced the man to go with him. On their way out of the parking lot, bullets from other warriors rained down on them. They did little damage to Savage, his vehicle, or his passenger.

They did manage to take out one target though. A semi-truck driver who had just turned into the place to fill up his truck. He was sitting up high enough so that one of the misguided bullets hit his windshield. It put a neat hole through the glass, hit him in the face, and killed him.

The truck continued moving and crashed into the gas pumps. Sparks flew and the now spraying fuel from the destroyed pump exploded. The chaos that followed ensured that no one would follow Savage and his passenger.

CHAPTER 8

Mack answered Lisa's call. "What's up?" he asked.

"I just wanted you to know what's going on. I'm with Dale, as you know. We're at the sheriff's office. Dale's not really up to talking much. He's just trying, right now, to deal with the day to day stuff. I'm going to stay here for the rest of the day. Just in case he needs someone to talk to, or maybe hold his hand. I suppose some people might wonder about that, but that's the least I can do for someone who's been such a good friend to all of us." She paused, and Mack could hear her heave a heavy sigh.

"But that's not the main reason I called. I think it would be best, if tonight we take Dale out somewhere. If nothing else, just to help him get through part of the night." She paused again, and again sighed heavily. "I also think you should bring Sue with you when you come. I know this might sound wrong. But if it does, please don't you take it wrong."

This time, Mack got almost a minute of silence. "If Sue's along," she said when she continued, "it will balance things out. There won't be anyone playing the fifth wheel."

"As in," Mack answered, "you don't want me to feel that way."

"Pretty much, yes."

"You know I do trust you, Lisa. And there's nothing that could ever make me stop loving you. But you are starting to sound like you are planing to take tonight beyond the boundaries of just a friendship. If you are, I won't stop you. I won't like it, but I won't tell you what you can do or not do. The thing is though, it will be difficult for me. If I know that's the plan, it might not hurt as much if I know ahead of time. Surprises like that are always tougher to handle."

"What you just said, Mack, is exactly what I meant when I asked you to not take it the wrong way. I'm disappointed that you did."

"There's a reason why I did. And you are definitely not it. I know you remember, when you and I started our current relationship, about Linda. I told you then, that things like this happen. And that it might happen to you. So I'm just trying to tell you, that if this is one of those times, I don't like it. But I do understand."

"You think you do, Mack. But right now, you aren't understanding. Please try to remember what happened to me when I was kidnapped. Because of that, I don't feel things the way I suppose other women do. I love you, beyond what you'll ever know. So I can be who I am with you. But no matter what, I could never be that woman with any other man. Remember that, when I act differently tonight. If you let us, you and I will always be you and I."

Mack didn't accomplish much the rest of the day. Sue readily agreed to accompany him for dinner with Dale and Lisa. Mack showered and shaved before they went out. He put on his best pair of Levis and a western style dress shirt.

Sue surprised him when she wore a semi' translucent red blouse, with a darker red bra under it. Her white skirt was full, and stopped about six inches above her knees. Her feet and legs were without stockings and her low heels were opened toed. She wore minimum makeup and her hair down over her shoulder's.

Mack's response when he saw her was an open mouth. She gave him a big grin. "I talked to Lisa," she simply said.

"Maybe," Mack answered, "but Lisa didn't do what I'm looking at. I've always thought you were beautiful, Sue. But now...now I no longer have the words to tell you what I think. *Wow!* You are something else."

When they met Dale and Lisa, Mack expected her to be wearing the same clothes she had on when they left the house in the morning. She wasn't. She was wearing a shimmering blue, rather low cut dress. It fit all of the contours and curves of her body perfectly. And like Sue's skirt, it was inches short of her knees. She had bought the dress that day, just for the evening. Mack was in one way, pleased that she took the time to make herself even ore beautiful than she normally was. It also filled him with a sense of being the second choice tonight. She'd bought and worn the dress for Dale.

When they were seated, unexpected to the rest of them, Lisa sat next to Dale. She wasn't particularly close, and didn't do anything through the meal that was at all improper. Yet, the arrangement made it feel to all four of them that it was Dale she was with, not Mack. It troubled her some though, that they didn't seem to understand why she was doing it.

Their conversation was intentionally light, so even though he was obviously down, Dale managed to contribute to it. The one thing that was noticeable was Sue. She sat across from Dale, and occasionally during the evening, if one of Dale's hands was close, she would reach out and touch it.

Initially, he shied away when she did it. But by the midpoint of the dinner, he appeared to be enjoying it. He was far more relaxed by the end of the meal than he was when it started. When they finished eating they moved to the bar area.

The music started soon after. Mack broke with what was happening through the evening. He asked Lisa to dance. Much to his surprise, she gave him a broad smile and said yes.

Once on the dance floor. as soon as he took her in his arms to a slow song, she said, "No, I'm not making a pass at Dale.

No, I am not going to spend the night with him. I have no desire to. When I planned this, I wanted it to be an evening that showed Dale that he is still very desirable to women. What he's going through now has got to be pure hell for him. His wife might have deserted him, but the rest of us never will. So stop your damn worrying, Mack Thomas. You are my man. The only man I want or ever will want. I'll be home with you tonight. It's just that, in the meantime, I want to help Dale feel better about himself."

When a fast song was played, they sat down. Dale and Sue left the dance floor at the same time. It was then that Mack, more than anyone else, noticed how crowded it was getting. And worse than crowded, it was becoming loud. Not a crowd friendly loud. A table of six, less than sober, loud and obnoxious men, were making a large portion of the noise.

As all too often happens, one of the men noticed Lisa and Sue. He pointed them out to the men he was with. They discussed them, softly enough so Mack and Dale couldn't hear their words. But the subject they were discussing was obvious. They kept pointing at Lisa and Sue.

It didn't take long for one of the men to get up and walk to their table. Sure he was big and macho enough to intimidate Mack and Dale, he had a smirk on his face. He immediately moved in on Lisa."

"I think you and I should dance a little," he said. He turned to Dale. "Now, you don't mind if this pretty gal dances with me some, now do you?" He tried to give Dale a look that told him he better not mind.

Dale surprised everyone when he instantly stood, facing the man. "I sure as hell do mind. So I think it best if you just back off. When she dances, she dances with me," he paused and pointed at Mack, "or him. No one else."

"Do you really think, asshole, that you can stop me from dancing with her if I really want to."

Before Dale could say anything, Lisa spoke up. "He not only can, he can easily do it. The truth is, I could too. So go sit down, before I'm forced to kick your sorry ass."

As stupid as the man was, he knew he better back off if he didn't want to get kicked out of the bar. Or worse than that, get the guys he was with kicked out too.

Mack was especially glad to see him go back to his table. Between what Wanda was going through, the trauma of Dale's split with Kathy, and his unexpected jealousy about Lisa, he'd had enough for one day.

They stayed at the bar for another hour. Before they left, Sue managed to get Dale out for two slow dances. Like Lisa, she wanted to make Dale feel good about himself. She made sure the dances were close enough so he would have no doubts about the woman he was holding. By then, Dale was still a long way from himself. But the fact he was facing a long night alone, the terror of it didn't loom as large as it might have without the support he'd received from all of them.

They walked to the parking lot together, but their vehicles were parked a ways apart. Lisa's pickup was still at the sheriff's office, so she was going to ride with Dale into Kingsburg to pick it up. Sue came there with Mack, so she was riding home with him.

Just as they were splitting up to go to their own cars, The five men from the bar walked into the parking lot. "Hey you," the man who was turned down for the dance yelled, "we want to talk to you." It was Dale that they wanted.

As they got close to Dale, the man stuck his face close to Dale's. "I didn't know who you was," he sneered, "the first time I saw you tonight. I do know now. I'm the foreman of the crew building the new sports center. You screwed us up royal when you run my men out of town. And for nothing too. So we are here to tell you, you'd best let them come back, or I'm gonna kick some ass."

"I really don't give a damn who you are," Dale answered. "Those men were going to rape five women. One of them was actually still a kid. Those men will never be welcome in this town again."

"Them goddamn women don't matter no how. My men knew about them. They was just whores. Whatever they would of got, they had coming anyway."

Mack moved up to the five men. He moved until he was inches from the man talking. "What did you call those women?' He used his shoulder to jar the man.

Lisa was watching and listening to Mack. The tone of his voice made her take a small gasp for breath. His now very pale complexion gave her a sudden sharp stabbing pain in her gut. He was on the edge and she knew it.

"Both of these women were there," Mack then said to him. "I think you'd best apologize to them." He moved his foot over the man's and twisted his own hard. The man was wearing work boots, but he felt it anyway.

"A whore is a whore, so hell no, I won't apologize. And if you don't back the hell off me right now, me and the boys here are gonna kick your ass. When we get done, we'll be treating these two whores the way they ought to be treated. We'll be ass fucking them until they bleed."

That was too much for Mack. He wouldn't have put up with that kind of talk anytime. But after the day he had, it set him off. His control was gone. He pushed the man hard, staggering him backward. Before he could regain his balance, Mack laid into him. He slammed him with two lefts on the side of his head. Then a right under the chin. His head snapped back and he went down.

Mack turned to the other four. "Either walk away, or you will get the same," he told them.

The men, who considered themselves to be the most macho of men, weren't able to consider backing down. Besides, they were four against two. Or so they thought. It never occurred to them that two women dressed the way these were, could possibly assist the men they were with in a fight. Of course, they were wrong. Lisa stepped in front of the first of the four to make a move.

He reached out with both hands to push her out of the way. She grabbed them, and as she used his momentum, she pulled him toward her, she kicked him in the groin with the pointed, high heeled shoes she was wearing. He doubled over and fell, landing hard on his nose. The heavy bleeding started right away.

The man who attacked Dale outweighed him by a good fifty pounds. He was stronger, but had the kind of build and muscles that left him with less agility than the average man. Dale used that to his advantage and quickly moved in on him. A series of powerful body punches slowed him close to a total stop. Dale them stepped back, and with a series of rapid blows to the man's head, knocked him out.

Mack and Lisa were dealing with the last two men by then. Mack was still close to as angry as it was possible for him to get. He played with his opponent unmercifully. He wasn't hurting him much physically, but he was coming close to killing the man's macho pride. Finally, Mack asked, "Enough?"

The man shook his head no. Mack shrugged, then hit him one more time. Knocking him out.

Lisa's man was a lousy fighter, and she quickly had him under control. She grabbed him between the legs and squeezed with everything she had in her. "You like raping women," she said as he screamed. "Well, I like wrecking men." She used a second hand to squeeze harder. He screamed louder. "You think about rape again," she let go of him, pushed him back some, and kicked what she stopped squeezing. "You think about what it feels like."

He first dropped to his knees, holding himself like he was afraid he'd lose something. Soon though, he rolled over on his side. Still holding on, he lay there moaning.

"Well," Dale said, "that about killed what was a good night."

"Are you going to arrest them, Dale?" Mack asked.

"Not tonight. I just plain don't feel like doing the paperwork. Let the bastards lay here. I'm not calling any ambulance for them either. They're on their own."

Dale and Lisa left for town then, so Lisa could get her pickup. Mack and Sue drove home. They didn't talk until they got there.

"I know," Sue said to him, "That today's been pretty hard on you. It wasn't hard to tell, from the look on your face, what was going through your mind. It takes a lot of man to do what you did for Dale today and tonight."

"I'm not so sure about that. I know I can trust Lisa. No matter what, she wouldn't ever leave me. So I really shouldn't have gotten jealous. It was stupid of me."

"No, Mack. It was real of you. It mostly just showed how much you love her. Now come. Walk me to my door."

It never occurred to Mack to ask her why she wanted him to do that. He should have wondered why though. She'd never done that kind of thing before.

When they reached her door, she turned to him, placed her hand behind his head and pulled him down. Their lips met, and she kissed him in a way he would never be able to forget.

After they broke it, she said, "That's for Lisa worrying you so much today. And just so you know, after that kiss, if things were different I'd drag you to my bed now and not let you go."

She took his hand, and held it to her breast for a moment. She kissed him again, turned away, and went inside.

He stood there for a couple of minutes, wondering about the way life kept shifting the course he thought he'd set for himself. He was still wondering as he sat in his favorite chair in the living room, while waiting for Lisa to get home. She wasn't far behind him.

"I'm so glad to be home," she said before she bent over and kissed him. "Home alone with my husband. Finally. I've been thinking all day, since I left the hospital, what I want to do with you."

She smiled and sat in his lap. "And now, I want to do it to you worse than ever. Sue texted me on the way home. She told me that it would be a good idea to take care of you tonight. Even if I am tired. Yes, I am jealous now too. She told me about the kiss. Let's go to bed. We have all night to make love. We can always sleep some other time."

And sleeping some other time is what it was going to be. By morning, Mack was wondering what the fuss was about. Why was he jealous. He couldn't even imagine how he and Lisa could ever reach the point Dale and Kathy did.

CHAPTER 9

Paul Danielson wanted to cover as much territory as possible, so he left home at a very early hour. His wife, being the supportive wife she now was, left the bed when he did. She kissed him goodbye, wished him well, and went back to bed. There was no need for her to stay up at that early of an hour.

Paul, on the other hand, felt a sense of urgency. The more he investigated the large numbers of dead cats and dogs, the more he realized how important it was to learn who was doing the killing. If for no other reason than to stop the cruelty involved.

His mission on this day was to check dumps near the western border of Minnesota. His hope was to find an end of dumps where dead animals were dumped. He knew that the farther away from the cities the problem was, the bigger the killing operation would turn out to be.

One of the major fears he, and all of the people in the Refuge Rescuers Agency had, was that the killing would spread into wildlife populations. Since whatever was killing the dogs and cats wasn't guns or other violent means, it was probably some kind of disease or poison. If it was disease that could kill both dogs and cats, it was possible it could affect other species too. With nearly all forms of wildlife being so rapidly depleted already, some new sickness or plague could be devastating.

He was about a hundred miles out, and the sun was up, when he emptied the last of the coffee in his insulated cup. He decided to stop in the next small town he came to, to get some breakfast and his cup refilled.

He found a real, old time cafe in the next town. Much better, in his opinion, than any fast food place. The food didn't have to be better for it to be better. For a middle aged man like Paul, it was the environment that mattered. This real cafe had a waitress who was well beyond her high school years, and a second one much younger. But young or not, she was filled with the small town, country girl enthusiasm. Her rosey cheeks, pig tails, and bright blue eyes gave her a beauty no amount of makeup could have created. Paul loved looking at her, and found the few freckles sprinkled over her cheeks and nose a thing of beauty.

He sat down at the counter, rather than a booth, when he went inside. He ordered the strong coffee from the older waitress, who in his opinion was also pleasing to the eye. After he ordered breakfast, he then looked at the Minneapolis morning paper that was lying on the other side of the counter.

When the waitress brought his food, he could tell from the looks of it that it would be good. The hash brown potatoes were fried on an aged griddle to a perfect golden brown. The over easy eggs came out of a shell, rather than scrambled and from a box the way they would at a fast food joint. The order of bacon was four crisp slices, and the toasted english muffin was loaded with real melted butter. All in all it more than satisfied a hungry man.

He pushed the paper aside and started eating when a man, who appeared to be around sixty, sat down next to him. "Mind if I look at the paper?" he asked Paul.

"Not at all. There's not much in there in the way of good news, but you're welcome to it."

The man smiled at Paul's answer. "I take it you aren't much happy with the way of the current world?"

"It's pretty much hard to be, given the way the country is being run lately."

"You're not a Trump fan?"

"You could pretty much say that, yes. It's hard to believe the amount of just plain illegal crap he's pulled."

"You a lawyer, that you know so much about the law?"

"No, not hardly. Given what I used to be, they often are not among my favorite people."

"That is probably a rather normal sentiment. I know it isn't any of my business, but I'm kind of a nosey old man. So let me guess about you. You are, or at least were, a cop."

"You guessed right. I'm a retired cop." Paul filled his mouth with a fork full of hash browns and egg.

"That's a career I think I might have liked. I'm a loan officer at the local bank. Started there right out of college. Not the most exciting way to make a living."

"I joined the Minneapolis Police Force at the same time in my life," Paul told him. "That's about the only work I've ever done."

"You look too young to be retired. I should think you'd miss being a cop. I'm not looking forward to retirement myself. I can't imagine spending every day home with my wife."

"I dreaded it too. But I got a chance to go to work for a county sheriff. After we left the big city, my wife and I started to get along better than anytime since the honeymoon. She no longer works a job. She stays home, and loves doing the domestic stuff. Who would have thought?"

"So, you're not really retired then? Now you're a deputy sheriff?"

Paul swallowed a mouthful of food. "I was, but I left that job too. Now, I actually work as a private detective."

The waitress came to get the man's breakfast order. He gave it to her before he answered Paul. "I kind of wonder why you'd do that? It's a bit of a step down, isn't it? Compare to being a real cop, I mean."

"I would have thought so at one time. But we don't do the kind of work where we try to get pictures of cheating wives or husbands. So far, just about all the cases we've been working on have been interesting. The one I'm working on now is more than interesting, it's downright weird."

"But it's probably something you're not allowed to talk about."

"Actually, I can talk about it. It isn't anything confidential. It has to do with dead animals."

"Really. Like someone's dog was murdered?"

"No. Much more than that. Someone's been dumping dead dogs and cats in dumps all the way from the cities to west of here."

"How do you know that? I can't see how you could know someone is dumping a few animals this far away from where you live."

"The thing is, it's more than a few animals. So far, we know about several hundred cats, and even more dogs. We were hired to find out who and why. We've gotten to the point that we'll continue to investigate it, even when our client can no longer pay us."

"I don't see how you could afford to do that, but it sounds like the right thing to do. Killing that many animals is downright cruel."

"It is, but it does fit in with the times. It seems to be getting harder to find much good in the world." Paul took his last bite of food and pushed his plate away.

"Well, some people are trying to do better." The man paused to organize what he was going to say. He wanted to tell Paul about something he considered good, but had to phrase it in such a way that it didn't disclose any private information. "Like I told you, I'm a loan officer at the local bank. I have a client I've given a few loans to, who is doing some good work for animals. Not everything is bad."

"That's nice to hear. The people we are looking for, might be doing something like that. But even if they are, they're killing to damn many animals to make it worth it."

"Well, I think the people I work with do use some dogs in their research, but I'm sure that's kept to a minimum."

Paul tried to smile at the words of the friendly man he was talking too. It came out a little bent. He waved at the waitress. When she came over he handed her his credit card and a twenty dollar bill. "The card is for the meal," he said. "The green is for you."

She responded with a smile.

After Paul left the cafe, he intentionally skipped a couple of dumps, so he could get farther west before the end of he day. His next few stops were the same as the others, no new information. Then came what would be the last one of the day. There he ran into some luck.

It was a small dump, with only two men working it. The man in the small shack who took the money from customers, said he didn't know anything. Not about finding dead dogs and cats. Not about anyone dumping them, even if someone had been.

The man working the dump itself was more helpful. "Yeah," he answered when Paul asked, "I've seen more dead dogs lately. A couple of bags of cats too. But given how people throw almost anything away, I never thought about it much."

"Did you ever see anyone do the actual dumping?"

"I did once. Some guy in a brown cargo van. It was a Ford, I think. But as much as most vehicles look alike nowadays, it's possible it was a different make."

"What did they dump?"

"A couple of German Shepards. And a bag of cats. I didn't count them."

"How long ago was it."

"I don't remember exactly. A week or two maybe."

"You didn't notice the license number, did you?"

The man laughed. "Not hardly. I had no reason to, at the time. If I see them again, I'll let you know. If you leave me a card or something."

"You didn't notice anything else about the van, did you?"

The man laughed. "Now that you asked, yes I did. There was a pretty good dent, just over the right rear tire. But that's all I can tell you." He got back on his machine and went to work.

Paul left the dump and headed for home. He stopped again, at the same cafe he was in that morning. He was surprised to see the banker sitting in almost the same place at the counter.

"Well, hello," the banker said when Paul sat down. "Did you solve your mystery today?"

"No such luck," Paul said. "As I suspected, the problem goes quite a distance though." He named the farthest town he was near. "I did pick up a little bit of information at the last dump though. For the first time, one of the guys working there saw someone making a dump. A couple of dogs and a bag of cats."

"Well," the banker said, actually sounding hopeful for Paul, "I hope he could identify the dumper for you."

"Not much there either. All he could tell me was that the dumper was driving a brown cargo van. It had a dent over the right rear tire."

The banker blanched slightly and turned his head away. It took him a moment before he faced Paul again. "That sure doesn't sound like much for you to go on."

"It isn't," Paul agreed, while making a note to ask Sue if she could check this banker out with her computer. He didn't bother to ask the man his name. He was a loan officer at the local bank, so he knew she would figure that out. He didn't ask, because he now suspected he knew something. If not, he wouldn't have reacted the way he did when Paul described the van.

Their conversation drifted off then, too other things. By the time Paul left, the banker was confident that Paul didn't pick up on it when he reacted to his mention of the van.

Paul did, however, stop a few miles up the road after he left the diner. He wrote everything he could remember from his conversation with the banker on his laptop. Then, to be safe, he did the same with everything that took place at the last dump he visited.

He was anxious to tell Mack and Lisa what he'd learned, and to get with Sue to start doing some searching for more information on her computer. But it was late when he finally got home, so he decided to do it in the morning.

CHAPTER 10

Paul gave Mack a call the first thing after he got up and finished his morning routine. Mack sounded groggy when he answered. "Sorry," Paul said, "did I wake you up?"

"You did." Mack laughed. "It's okay. Lisa and I had another late night last night, and we've already overslept."

Paul chuckled. "Sounds like things are good with you two now."

"They couldn't be better. So what can I do for you?"

"I finally learned a little bit yesterday. So I have a couple of leads for Sue to check out. I think you, Lisa, Sue, and I should get together this morning. Where do you want to meet?"

"Like always, dad and Theresa will be making breakfast. So let's meet there. Hopefully, I'll be able to get Lisa up and ready by the time you get here."

Paul couldn't hold back another chuckle. As good as he and his wife got along now, it was a long time since they'd had the same wonderful problem Lisa and Mack were now having. "Your dad's place for a meeting sounds good. I assume that Sue will be there."

"She usually is, and I don't know of any reason she won't be today."

They hung up and Mack woke Lisa. She smiled at him when she opened her eyes. "Time to get up," he said. "Paul's got some things to talk about dealing with the dead critters. He's on his way to dad's. So you'd best get up and dressed.

She frowned. "I was thinking about something way different when you woke me up." She winked and her smile came back. "I don't suppose we could try and fit it in now, could we."

"We could if we really wanted to. Trouble is, I'm not built like you, so my recovery time is longer. And morning now or not, it hasn't been long since the last time. So let's go have breakfast and find out what Paul has to say. Maybe we can come back home after."

"Well, okay." She threw back the covers and got out of bed.

As Mack watched her naked body move while she picked up her robe, he thought that maybe things could be worked out right then after all. But once she covered herself with the robe, he again managed to take control of his own desires. As much as he knew he'd enjoy it, he forced himself to let it go until later.

They managed to get to Ben's before Paul. But not before Roy, Sue, or even Julie. Roy couldn't help but laugh lightly when they went in. He stared at Lisa and shook his head. "Wanda's coming home today," he said, but continued to stare hard at Lisa.

Mack couldn't help but wonder what it was about Lisa that Roy was reacting too. It seemed to Mack that he should be thinking more about Wanda. Nor could he pick up on why everyone else looking at her and smiling. Lisa looked just fine to him. Her clothes were nothing special. She was pretty much dressed like Mack. A western cut blouse, a pair of blue jeans with a somewhat tight fit, and western boots.

What the other's picked up on that Mack missed, was the look on her face. It was one of a woman who couldn't be more satisfied and happy. With her life, what it was, and most of all, what it had been a good part of the previous night. It was a glow she emitted that made everyone who saw her feel better. They knew from it, that there were good things that went way beyond the normal trials and strife.

Lisa then caught the look in Roy's eyes. She smiled at him and said, "Yes, Roy, it was that good."

His return laughter was infectious, and everyone joined him in it. Even Mack. Lisa didn't laugh. She simply smiled. And even though it was the kind of thing that would make most people blush, she didn't. Instead, she rode through it with a look of pride. And before the laughter stopped, she kissed her husband. With a kiss that showed she meant it.

That quieted the laughter, and after a moment of silence, the conversation around the table returned to normal. Paul arrived then too, so after the normal greetings, Mack started with the first question.

"As I'm sure you know, we are really curious about what you learned yesterday. So what was it?"

"Like I told you, I learned a little bit. Not near as much as I'd have like to, but a little. It was at my last stop, checking on the dumping. The guy there who was running the moving machine, said he saw a dumping."

"Did he get a license number?"

"No, nothing that good. All he gave me was a description of the cargo van they were in. He thought it was probably a Ford, but couldn't guaranty that. It was brown, and had a significant dent over the right wheel."

"That's it? That's next to no help at all." Mack shook his head with his disappointment.

"I know that alone is next to nothing, but there is a side story to that. It does have some potential." Paul told them then about the banker. How their conversation began. What they talked about the first time. Especially about the banker mentioning a client who was doing something for animals, who used dogs research. It wasn't until he explained about the banker's reaction to Paul's description of the van, that got them all talking about the significance of what Paul learned.

Sue finally called a halt to the speculations about the banker. "I think," she told them, "we should check the banker out before continue this conversation. All of his relevant clients too. There's no telling how far that might take us."

"Are you going to be able to do that, Sue?" Lisa asked. "When the only thing you know for sure is the name of the town where the banker works."

"Sure. In a town that size, there isn't likely to be anymore than one bank. So I can find who I'm looking for by checking on the bank's loan officers. I can pinpoint the one we want by age. If there's more than one that could fit the description, I'll check them both out. Worse come to worse, I'll end up searching the DMV for driver's license photos. When we nail it down to our guy, I'll check on his clients at the bank. I should be able to learn quite a bit about them, but not everything you want to know. You guys will have to do some hands on checking to learn everything you want. If, that is, I find any clients who seem at all suspicious."

Ben and Theresa started serving breakfast then. As they started to eat, Roy began talking about something that was bugging him. "Did any of you see the latest news about that Savage Strange jerk?"

"I think we all probably have," Mack said, between bites of smoked sausage that he was eating. "The latest about him has been on all the news."

"It sure has," Roy said. "This time, he got his daughter killed. He did one thing though, that wasn't all bad. He took the man who did it as a hostage. The thing is," Roy paused and looked around the able. "They haven't caught him yet."

"And you have what on your mind because of that?"

"Everything dealing with him and what he's done. If he isn't caught by the time Wanda feels up to doing it, I want to do something that isn't something we've ever talked about doing."

"That sounds radical, Roy," Mack said. "But radical is okay sometimes. So fill us in."

"I want to approach Savage Strange's dead wive's family. I want to offer our services pro bono, and go after him. He needs to be caught and locked up for the rest of his life. I know, this is the kind of thing we would normally leave to the police. But there's something about this case that gives me the feeling they need our help. Besides that, I have to admit that what he did to his wife and daughter really, really pisses me off. Not to mention, he did shoot Wanda."

"What makes you think we can find him if the police can't?"

"We can do things the police aren't allowed to do. Put Sue to work on it for one. We don't have to be so exact when we explain to a judge where we might have gotten our information. We can go places and check things without waiting for a bunch of paperwork. And we'll be doing something we want to do it. Not mostly because it just happens to be part of our job."

"Who's going to work the case?"

"Me and Wanda mostly. Paul, but only when or if you aren't using him for your animal case. And Sue, of course, for the technical stuff."

"I don't have any problem with you doing it," Mack told him. "But since it is a radical idea, I think we need to take a vote on it. And even though Wanda isn't here this morning, there are enough of us partners to vote. So everyone who approves of Roy's proposal, raise your hand."

Every hand in the room went up, even from those not partners. Roy's proposal was passed.

They went back to eating, and their conversation reverted to talk of the weather, Ben's vegetable crops, and Theresa's work at the community garden she managed.

Just before they were about to break up their breakfast meeting, Lisa mentioned Dale, wondering how he was doing.

"He stopped by for a while yesterday," Ben said. "He is definitely a man in a world of hurt. It sure is a hard thing, trying to understand what made Kathy do what she did."

Lisa looked a Mack. "It sounds like I put you through a lot of worry for nothing. I was really hoping that I helped him some."

"You did, Lisa," Sue explained. "I saw him as he was leaving here. He told me to tell you, that what you did meant the world to him. Without it, life would be a lot harder to deal with."

"Good. I'm glad I could help him get through the pain he must be feeling. He's such a good man. He deserves whatever any of us can do for him, or give him."

Looking at them, Mack momentarily wondered how far Lisa and Sue would, if it came down to it, be willing to take that idea. In Lisa's case, he didn't know how he would deal with the answer, what ever the answer was. But he also knew that it was highly unlikely there would ever be the question. So he did his best to shut his foolish thoughts down. He needed to concentrate on the real work to be done.

CHAPTER 11

Wanda was ready to leave the hospital when Roy got there. He was all smiles when he found her already dressed and waiting for the mandatory wheel chair to take her out the door to be loaded in the car.

"If you're parked in the lot," she told him, "you can go get the car right now. I'll signal the nurse to take me out."

Roy's mile just broadened farther as he left to get the car. It was Wanda's, and he didn't particularly like driving it. He much preferred his pickup. But the car was easier for Wanda, with her still painful wounded side, to get in and out of.

She was there, waiting in a wheelchair, when he stopped in front of the hospital's main entrance. The young man behind the wheelchair took the time to carefully assist her when she got up and moved to sit down in the car.

"You be careful now, Mrs. Thomas," he said as he backed away with the chair. "And have a good day."

Roy couldn't help but comment about him. "He looks awful young to be a nurse."

"He's not a nurse," Wanda answered. "He's a volunteer. There's actually quite a few of them working in the hospital now. They seem to be more helpful than what can be normally expected from kids their age. Watching them, during the short time I was there, made me feel just a little bit better about the future."

"They must be doing a hell of a good job then. It's damn hard to find anything, the way things have been going since all the Republicans turned into Fascists, to be positive about."

"I know, Roy. But I can always find something good in life. Just being with you and part of your family is often enough. And best of all, without bringing more babies into an already overcrowded world, that family is growing."

"You mean Sue." Roy blushed slightly when he used her nane. Something he recently had become prone to do.

"Yes, I was referring to her. But I was also thinking that there was someone else we should do our best to at least make him feel like family."

"That can only be Dale. The thing is though, don't we already do that?"

"To some extent. He knows that all of us consider him a friend. We should do what we can to make him feel that he's more than that. Like he's your brother and I'm his sister."

"I can't argue that, but at the same time, we do have to be careful that too much isn't given to him." Roy went on to tell her about the day Lisa put Mack through more misery than what was necessary. "She meant well, and had no wish to do that to Mack. But she did."

"Are they okay now?"

"Oh yeah." He smiled, thinking about Lisa's look that morning. "You know Mack. He'd have forgiven her even if she'd carried her trying to help Dale way too far. And Lisa, well, when she realized how Mack was effected, has been making it up to him ever since."

"And how," Wanda asked, "would you know that?"

"The way they look. When you next see them, you too will know."

"Knowing those two, I don't doubt it."

Not yet sure how Wanda felt physically, Roy was somewhat hesitant to talk about the Savage Strange case. At the same time, he knew better than anyone, that she hated it when people put off talking about things that needed talking about. So he told her about it and what he wanted to do.

Her eyes brightened as he talked. By the time he finished telling her about the case, she was enthusiastically nodding her head. He turned his head from the road to give her a quick look. She smiled.

"What do you think about the idea?" he asked, hoping for an affirmative answer.

"It's got one major flaw," she said. "And if you leave that one flaw in your plan, our chances of solving the case are much less."

"All plans are imperfect," he argued. "So I don't doubt that this one is too. But I don't see any major flaws in it."

"I didn't figure you would. Because the main reason for the flaw is me. As always, you are overly concerned about me. Another reason is the police. But we can work around them if they don't want to work with us."

"That's fine, but that still doesn't tell me the major flaw."

"I thought it did."

"I doesn't."

"It's damn well obvious enough. The flaw is in waiting. We have to get started on it today. And we can best do that by checking with Sue as soon as we get home. The first thing we need to do is figure out who in the wife's family to contact first."

"I already have an ida about that. She had a sister. She might be the best one to start with.'

"Do you have a number for her, Roy?"

"Not yet. Sue can find it for us."

"Okay. And as soon as we have it, I can call her. You can continue to go over what we need with Sue. We definitely want to stop that guy before he starts anymore trouble, or hurts anyone else."

"Okay, Wanda. We'll go ahead with this. As long as you're sure you're up to it."

"I still hurt some, but not enough to hold me back from moving ahead on this. We really need to catch this guy and get him locked up. Otherwise he will hurt someone else."

They contacted Sue as soon as they got home. She managed to put what she was working on aside for a couple of hours. They then set to work. Wanda was pleased that Roy was willing to start immediately, instead of waiting until she healed some more. It did give them a better chance to catch Savage. Unfortunately though, not before he decided he needed to go out again.

Savage Strange wanted to shop for more food. Things that were simple to prepare. He was pretty much useless when it came to anything involving work in the kitchen. He also hoped he could disguise himself well enough to play a few hands of blackjack at the casino. He just knew he was due to win big. After all, he couldn't lose forever.

His biggest problem now, was his hostage, a one Harold Cramer. A man he hated with a deep abiding passion. It wasn't only that he'd killed his daughter with his wild shooting. He had tried to shoot Savage. Now that was a grave sin if there ever was one.

Savage gave Harold a look of scorn. "I'm going to be leaving for a few hours," he said. "what should I do with you while I'n gone?"

"Untie me," Harold answered, his voice barely above a whimper. "I won't go nowhere."

"I can't hardy do that. We both know you'd try to escape."

"No, I wouldn't. I swear I wouldn't. I don't have the slightest idea where I am. So I wouldn't know where to go. And my hand hurts so bad, I don't think I can walk anyway."

"It hurts that bad, huh?"

"Yes, it does."

That gave Savage an idea. Which was something. It was generally difficult for him to get even small ideas on his own. He untied Harold from the chair and told him to lie on the floor. He was more than happy to do it. To be free from his ropes was an immense relief.

That relief was very short lived. Savage quickly shot him in both feet. "I don't guess you'll be running anywhere now will you?"

Harold didn't answer. He was too busy screaming. When he stopped, he cried. And moaned.

Savage laughed at him. "I think," he said, "my kid would like watching you now. If she was still alive." But Savage didn't actually care what she would think. For him, she was more of a burden than something he could care about. What he cared about now was going to the casino. He needed to get into the action. For him, gambling was incredibly exciting. And with his limited mental capacity, even more exciting than being hunted by nearly every police officer in Minnesota.

But first, he needed to get his hands on some more cash. He just didn't have enough for laying down any serious bets. So the question was, who should he rob first?

As he drove through the first town located on the lightly traveled state highway he took to get to the four lane the casino was on, he noticed the bank. It was in a small building, and gave him the feeling that it would be easier to rob than even the typical service staton. There would be far fewer people to deal with in the bank.

So he only drove a short distance before he turned around. He backed into the parking spot right in front of the bank. It made it easier to make a quick getaway. Inside, there were no customers. One female teller was on duty. Two men, each in their own glassed office, appeared to be busy with something on their computers.

He quickly decided that the best way to keep things simple was to shoot the two men right away. The woman would be easier to deal with when she was alone. As far as he was concerned, women were always easier to deal with if they were scared. If he shot the men, he was sure it would scare her. It never occurred to him that shooting the men might have some ramifications on what he was trying to do.

So he did. In the head, killing them both. She screamed, fainted, and fell to the floor. He quickly revived her and got her on her feet.

"Empty your cash drawer," he told her. Without any argument, she did what he asked. When the drawer was empty, he said, "Now the safe."

In a voice so shaky he had a hard time understanding her, she explained, "I can't. They always keep it locked so we don't get robbed. Only the bank manager has the combination. And you shot him."

Savage walked her to the safe anyway. "Open it," he again ordered.

"I really can't," she said, bowing her head in fear.

"You really, honestly can't open the damn thing?"

"No," she said again. About that time they heard the first of the distant sirens.

"Did you set off the alarms?"

"They went off automatically when I emptied the cash drawer."

"I think you're lying to me. I hate it when people lie to me."

"I'm not. It really is automatic for the police to be called. I'm too scared to do something like that."

He shook his head in disgust. The sirens got louder. He decided that he had no choice. It was time to get the hell out of there. But he wasn't wearing a mask, so he decided he had only one choice. He put the gun to her head and pulled the trigger. The way he did it was a mistake. When her head exploded, it covered his face with her blood and tissue. Generous amounts of it also landed on his shirt. A small piece of bone stuck in his forehead.

Now his explosive temper went off. He looked around for someone to hurt. But everyone other than him in the bank was dead. So he reluctantly left the bank, got in his car, and drove away. There would be no visit to the casino on this day. Since he was covered with blood and other parts of the teller, he was sure he'd be noticed there. On the highway, he drove by the first cop car as it drew close to the bank.

He would have turned around and gone to the bank, so he could shoot them, if he dared. But they carried guns, and he was afraid that he might get shot. And that wasn't something he was prepared to do. Getting shot pretty much scared him. So he continued back to the shabby cabin he was staying in.

"At least," he thought, "this time he wouldn't get the blame for what happened at the bank. All the witnesses were dead."

He was wrong. The bank was full of security cameras. All of them in good working order. By the time the evening local news cycle started, the media was filled with details about the robbery and the killings. They also filled the television screens with photos taken during Savage's botched robbery and murders. There was now a huge manhunt out for him that was being taken seriously by law enforcement.

He was also being heavily covered by the media now. Roy and Wanda went over everything they'd learned from Sue's research on Savage, as they listened to the news.

"It's beginning to look less likely all the time," Roy said as they watched, "that with us officially having the case now or not, we will ever need to go after him."

"You're kind of disappointed about that, aren't you, Roy?"

"Some, I guess. But not so much I don't want to see him caught. If they catch him, him being caught is what matters most."

"But if they don't, you still want to go after him? Even after all the people he's murdered?"

"I do, Wanda. I won't though, if you're against it now."

"No, Roy, I'm not. What good are we, if we can't go after the bad guys just because they're a little dangerous."

"Good. I'm glad you feel that way. I think I'll go through this stuff from Sue one more time. Just in case I can find something we can use."

He went through the pile of things she'd printed out for them, one piece at a time. Near the bottom of the pile, he found the title of a piece of land that was set back, far off any kind of main road. The first name on the title wasn't Savage. But the last name was Strange.

Roy set it aside. It wasn't likely to be relevant, but might prove to be worth checking if Savage wasn't found and arrested. There was one other thing that was interesting to Roy. The land was located in the same area as the bank that was just robbed. Too much of a coincidence to ignore.

When Roy gave up on the pile. At least for that day, he hadn't found anything to tell him specifically where to look. In fact, the relatively obscure deed was the best lead they had, should they ultimately need one.

He took it to Sue, and from the property description on the title she got an address for the property. Even better, she also set Roy up with the GPS coordinates.

CHAPTER 12

Kathy was excited and nervous. The same way she was before every concert, but especially the first concert of a tour. As always, she was getting a lot of support from everyone. Especially the man in charge of the equipment and the rest of the road crew in general.

Terrance Withers loved being in charge. And on this trip, he was loving it even more than usual. This time she was free of her damn sheriff husband. This time she was his. He'd wanted her for a long time, but she'd always resisted. Tonight, he was sure, would be different. Tonight, for the first time, he would prove that he was the better man. And then, she was his. He would be in charge. He would, in fact, own her.

Kathy too, could feel that tonight would be different. She had strong feelings for Terrance, and tonight she might let some of those feelings show. She didn't think though, that she was ready to take those feelings as far as he wanted to. Not yet, anyway.

But first, and more importantly, was the concert. She knew she was ready, and wanted to make it the best she'd ever done. She was on her own now. Alone. Without Dale's support. So she would need to be the best. He was no longer available to get her through the trauma if anything was to go wrong. In the past, no matter what time it was for him. Or how far away she was, he was always there for her if she needed him. He was always there, even if all she wanted to do is tell him how the concert went. And he always listened.

But now she had Terrance. And he was a right here. Not far away. He could, she was sure, be her rock, her full support, should she need it. He loved the tour, the crowds, and the celebrations when things went right. Dale didn't. So now Dale was gone, and she had Terrance.

At show time, while she waited to make her entrance, he stood beside her holding her hand. When the music started and it was time to go on stage, he kissed her first. A kiss he was sure would tell her who she belonged to now. She didn't much like it that he did that when he did. It took something away from her concentration.

But she shook it off as she walked out to meet her audience. Her face was filled with a brilliant smile as the lights came on. The auditorium was filled with applause, whistles, and cheers as soon as the people in the seats saw her. Just as quickly, it became quiet as she started her first song. Only her voice, music from the band, and flashes from a couple thousand cameras filled the place.

The applause at the end was near deafening. For a little more than two hours, many thousands of people did nothing but sit and love watching Kathy sing. Some cheered so loud they became unable to make a sound, even before the music was over.

When she completed her last song, said thank you to the grateful audience, they stood as one and gave her an ovation like she'd never before seen. She bowed, covered her hands with her face, and cried. She was thrilled with their response, but more than that, she was grateful for it. When it was finally all over, she rushed to her dressing room. She closed the door and immediately found her cell phone. She called Dale. She had to share the awesome night she'd had with him. The same way she always did. It wasn't until she was about to push the last number that she remembered. There no longer was a Dale. Unexpectedly to her, her heart fell as she hung up the phone.

Still holding the phone, she sat down on the only chair in the room. She tried hard to regain the jubilation she felt when the concert ended, but it was gone. She sat still then. Staring at the wall, but seeing nothing. Wondering why she now felt so down, so lost.

Terrance entered the room, looking at her as if she'd committed some kind of great sin against him. "What's the phone for?" he asked, his voice angry. "Did you call your husband the way you always used to?"

Without looking at him, she answered, "No. I haven't called anyone."

"Well, you damn well better not have. You are mine now, so you have to do any celebrating with me. No one else."

"I'm not celebrating. I don't feel very good right now. I want to change. Give me a few minutes, and I'll come out and join all of you in your celebration."

"What the hell do you mean, Kathy? Give you a few minutes?" He moved behind her, bent over, and kissed her neck.

With her down mood dominating her, she didn't respond to him. But she didn't do anything to push him away either. Nor did she as he continued to kiss her. She let him stand her up and lead her to the narrow cot at the back of the room.

She felt empty as he unzipped the back of her gown, and barely noticed as he slipped it off her shoulders. She was left then, with only panties and her bra on.

He undressed, and that was when she finally realized what was actually happening. She turned her head away when he tried to kiss her again. He held her chin so he could kiss her.

"Like I keep telling you," he hissed between clenched teeth. "You're mine now."

He kissed her, then moved his hands behind her and unhooked her bra. He let it fall to the floor. She moved her hands over her breasts, wanting to keep them covered. Doing that left her open enough for him to pull down her panties.

She crossed her legs when he pushed her down on the cot. She knew she should fight him off. Scream if she had to. Somehow stop him. She didn't. She gave up then and let it happen. The physical part of her wanted to respond to him. She didn't hate what he was doing. Only what was happening to her. Dale's face flashed through her head. She knew then, that this was the worst, most stupid thing she'd ever done.

She was cheating. Cheating with a man who now thought he owned her. No one owned her. Dale had never tried. All he ever did was love her. Something, she knew now, Terrance never would. He wasn't, she now realized, capable of it.

Without moving, with only a slow, soundless breathing, she let him finish with her. When he was done, she violently pushed him away and escaped the cot.

"Get the hell out of here," she demanded.

"Not on your life," he argued, a sneer on his face. "After what I just gave you, you got to know you belong to me. I know damn well you ain't never had it like that before."

"You are right. I never have. Nothing so dirty has ever been done to me before."

"The hell. You loved it. Your hillbilly cop husband never could have done what I done. Women always tell me they love what I do to them."

"I didn't. I hated what you did. I hated why you did it. And most of all, I hated how you did it. Not get the hell out of this room. Now! You don't, and I will scream rape. Who do you think will be believed if I do that?"

Terrance lifted his hand as if to hit her, but quickly thought better of it. Even his road crew were more loyal to her than they were to him. He started to get dressed.

"One more thing, Terrance," Kathy said. "I belong to no one, and if you come near me again, first I scream, then at minimum, I fire you. So plan on staying the hell away from me."

Kathy sat on her bed in her hotel room for a long time before falling asleep that night. All she could do is wonder how she could have done such a good job of screwing up her life. She had a long tour ahead of her. What would become of her life when it was over. Was what she'd get from this tour be worth what she was sure she will have lost when it was over. She now doubted it.

The city they were in was scheduled for a double concert. Kathy was thankful for that, because after a very restless night, she got some extra needed rest.

The second concert was as successful as the first. Even if they did have constant lighting problems throughout it. The music, especially her voice, held it together. The audience loved her. And as it was the first time, she received a standing ovation at the end.

The concert was followed by frantic packing and loading the bus. In a couple of hours, they were on the road to the next concert. The trip wasn't as bad as some. It was only a little over five hundred miles.

Terrance approached Kathy around the halfway point. She was awake, so before he could sit down next to her, she shook her head no and waved him off.

The rest of the time before the start of the next concert was uneventful. But when the concert started, they immediately had problems with the microphones.

After a couple of attempts to sing, Kathy called it to a temporary halt until the problem was repaired. As soon as she did, the youngest member of the road crew approached her.

"I know," he told her, "who did this. I guess Terrance will fire me for this, but he caused the problem. He didn't know I was watching him when I was."

"Don't worry," she answered. "You won't be fired." She already suspected Terrance of being the problem. She found him playing with one of the cables. "Pack your personal things and get the hell out of here. Right now. You are fired."

"You can't do that. I'll take the whole road crew with me."

"Go ahead, if you can. You are fired anyway."

Terrance tried to talk the road crew into leaving with him. To a man, they refused. "Bitch. You are a goddamn bitch!" he swore at her as he left.

The crew soon got the microphones working again, and Kathy went back on stage. She sang her heart out and the concert proved to be a big success. Another standing ovation.

They had no more equipment problems. But they had one big problem only Kathy knew about. After every concert, she felt worse. She couldn't get past wondering why she did what she did. It was the worst at the end of each concert. She desperately needed someone to share her feelings with. But because of her stupidity and arrogance, the one she needed was no longer there for her.

CHAPTER 13

Sue continued her searches on her computer for any information she could find concerning the ever rising number of dead dogs and cats. Long before she finished, she had enough to send Mack and Lisa out checking on leads.

One of their first stops was at a huge store specializing in animal feed and other animal products, which they sold both wholesale and retail. Mack and Lisa started with the manager of the store. They were honest when they introduced themselves and told him why they were there.

He wasn't inclined to answer their questions. "That kind of information is, as it ought to be, confidential."

"The thing is," Lisa said, using her sweetest voice, "there are a lot of innocent animals dying who probably shouldn't. Given their numbers, it amounts to cruelty that goes beyond normal imagination."

"I can't help that none. The customers deserve their privacy. And I...we, don't know for sure what you are really going to do with that kind of information. With the economy the way it is, everyone's looking for more business. On the chance you might be a competitor, I can't afford to steer you to my customers."

His attitude frustrated them, but they couldn't blame him for it. They left him and went inside the store. They purchased several bags of dog food.

A young clerk from the store helped Mack load it onto the back of his pickup.

"Things must be slow for you guys lately," Mack said as they worked. "It's usually a lot more crowded when I'm here."

"Yeah, the store is slower, but business isn't as bad as it seems. We've got a fairly new customer that buys hundreds of bags of dog and cat food. And from what I've heard, all of our stores in the midwest have customers like that."

"Is it the same customer?" Mack asked. "Or does each store have a different customer?"

"I have no idea. I just know that whoever it is, they are the main reason I still have a job."

"Do you ever wonder what it is they are doing, that they use so much dog food?"

"Not really. I don't care what they're doing with it. Or why they need it. I only care that I still have a job. The money I make is what's important. Nothing else."

They finished loading the dog food, and the young man went back inside the store. Mack and Lisa left, and drove straight to the local animal rescue facility. They normally were happy to receive food donations. This time, they were shaking their heads when Mack told them what they had.

The manager of the place said, "We have no idea what's going on. But rather than being way over crowded the way we've been for more years than I care to think about, we're only about half full right now."

"Really?" Lisa answered him. "How long has the been going on?"

"I'm not sure exactly. I started noticing that fewer strays and such were being brought in about a year ago. Almost no dogs or cats have been brought in, in the last six months. Even the local kitten population seems to have disappeared."

"Do you have any idea why?"

"Not for sure. I've heard that there's some big corporation that's buying a lot of cats and dogs. But I don't know how true that is. None of us here know what the company might be doing with it either."

Even though they didn't really need it, the rescue people accepted the food anyway. The fact that the rescue place had far fewer animals to take care of, told Mack and Lisa that there was probably some kind of connection between the dead dogs and the lack of rescue dogs. Either way, it seemed as though the animal control people should be noticing the changes too. And since they'd shown an interest in the dead dogs, even before Refuge Rescuers were involved, they decided to pay them a visit.

The response they got from them was far less than encouraging. The lead person at their office, when Mack and Lisa went in, declined to answer any questions."

"You know, don't you," Mack said, "that not answering any questions at all, tells me that you are trying to coverup something. It seems to me, that you should be concerned about dead animals turning up in the numbers that they have."

"What concerns us right now is you two. The last thing we need around here is a couple of crackpots making ridiculous claims about animals being killed. If there was a problem, we would be taking care of it. So please, go home and let us professionals deal with the animals. That's what we're here for." With that, he turned his back.

Mack and Lisa gave up on those people then. At least for the day. It made no sense to waste any more time with them, when they now had so many leads to follow up on. Especially people who seemed to think keeping secrets made them more powerful. Even though their secrets were not necessary, and were possibly harmful.

Since it was now apparent that the dead animal dumping was affecting everyone dealing directly with or handling products for cats and dogs. They decided a visit to a veterinarian might prove fruitful. Their choice of a vet was easy to make.

It was only a matter of months since they started Refuge Rescuers. Prior to that, Mack and Lisa were partners with Roy and Wanda in the cattle business. Their herd consisted breeding cows who were permanently part of the herd, and several hundred steers they fed out until they were ready for shipping.

The vet they decided to stop and see was the one who supervised the health care of that herd. So they at least started out on a good footing this time, when they stopped to talk to her.

"I can't tell you much," she answered when they asked her about all the dead dogs and cats. "To tell you the truth, I didn't know the problem was so large or so widespread. I do some work with small animals like dogs and cats, but the bulk of my business is with beef cattle, dairy cows, and of course, horses. As far as dogs and cats, I've unsuccessfully treated a few isolated animals. They died rather quickly of something I couldn't pinpoint. It was a rather painful death. I think it was some kind of virus. That's all I know."

"Do you have any guesses as to what it might be?"

"Just one. It is probably something new. Where it came from, or could have come from, is something else I don't know. My gut feeling though, is that it's probably a good thing you guys are looking into it. If I had time, I would. But right now, I just don't have any extra time."

They went back home then, with the feeling that they'd fallen into a mystery far more serious than they thought it was when they decided to take it on.

They stopped to see Sue when they got there. The first thing they had her do was get into the sales records of the feed store where they purchased the dog food. Because they'd broken down the sales of both dog and cat food by brand, it took a while to evaluate the records. Once they did, it clearly showed that the biggest sales were to a multibillion dollar drug corporation. But the amount of food they were buying didn't correspond with the number of dead animals.

They decided there could be two reasons for that. The most obvious being the fact they were buying food from more than one company. The other was, the animals they were feeding weren't living long enough to eat much. It was also possible both reasons were involved in what was going on.

Another problem was the question. Why would a giant, extremely rich, drug company be killing dogs and cats in large numbers. Somehow, it just didn't compute. It made no sense that they would be involved in something like that. They were already taking in record profits by ripping off millions of diabetics with their over pricing of insulin. Not to mention the dozens of other over priced drugs they manufactured and sold.

It wasn't until Sue checked out the deliveries of the pet food that they decided to check out the places that received it. There were nearly a dozen of them. They were scattered around three states,, with slightly over half of them in Minnesota. The rest were in South Dakota and Wisconsin.

Sue printed out the addresses, and they decided to do at least a drive by of one that day. They found it located in a wooded area northwest of Kingsburg a few miles.

It was a plain, unpainted concrete block building. It was surrounded by a chain link fence which ran around it, about thirty-five feet from it. That fence was surrounded by another fence, which ran around at about a hundred feet away from the building. The picture it made was very much like that of a prison.

Somewhere between every twenty to thirty feet, large keep out signs were hung on the outside fence. Just inside the main gate a guardhouse held a man in uniform. Hanging from and extra belt low on his waist was a large caliber pistol, a flashlight, a club, and a can of pepper spray in a special holster.

Mack and Lisa made the decision to not approach the place then. They knew it would be a good idea to learn a lot more about what was going on before attempting to get inside the place.

Instead, since it was still too early in the day to do it, they called Paul Danielson. He was again checking out the dumps in the western part of the state. They gave him the address of the animal delivery drop, and suggested he check it out on his way home.

It was far enough out of his normal route home, so he decided to quit his dump research early. Using GPS, he had little trouble finding the place. It was nearly identical to the one Mack described to him. One difference was a road that wound around it. A road he followed.

He nearly missed it, and was passed it when he did see it. He backed up some then, to get a closer look. The building was small, and located on the far side of the road from the fenced in facility. The sign on it said Jabber Research. Parked in front of it was a brown, Ford cargo van. It had a large dent above the right rear wheel.

"Now we're getting somewhere," he told himself as he wrote down the license number of the van. "Finally, we have something solid to go on." As he drove away, he made a mental note to check with Sue, to see what she'd learned about the banker. He knew that it was more than possible that Jabber Research, whatever it was, could be the company he said he borrowed money to.

When Paul got back to Kingsburg, it was too late in the day to get together with everyone, so he decided to go over what he'd learned during breakfast in the morning.

CHAPTER 14

Roy was getting ever more restless every day. They always had simpler cases to deal with then the hundreds of dead animals case, or killers like Savage Strange. So it wasn't that he and Wanda didn't have anything to do working on the simpler cases. It was far more like he needed a bigger challenge. The simple things he faced in life, no matter what they were, sometimes just weren't enough to hold his attention.

This morning was definitely one of those times. The simpler cases he was handling weren't demanding enough of him. What he wanted now was something more difficult, more challenging. And the Savage Strange case was that. As near as he could tell, the police were at a standstill with him. They didn't appear to be at all close to catching and arresting him.

That meant Roy was anxious to be the one to bring him in. He was sure, and his gut feeling agreed with what was in his head, that the man was staying on that property out in the woods.

Since he and Sue took their original look at it, they'd taken a second look. This time, she found the satellite photos of it. It was difficult to see, because of the tree cover, but there was definitely a small cabin there. It looked old and weathered in the photo, but still whole. And even if it was a rather uncomfortable place to live in, it could still be a good place for Savage to hide out. Especially when every law enforcement organization in the state was hunting him.

Roy did his best to notify the FBI and the state police about the cabin. They just told him to stick with domestic problems and leave the real police work to them. They didn't need any meddling from know nothing amateurs.

That, of course, rankled Roy to no end. It left him wanting more than ever to go after Savage. And that was what he wanted to talk about at breakfast.

He was going to have a hard time dominating the conversation though. Paul, Mack, and Lisa needed to discuss the animal case. And in reality, Sue had something every bit as important to talk about. The good friend to all of them. Sheriff Dale Magee.

As he so often did though, Roy still managed to open the conversation. He did it with two words. "Savage Strange." He looked around the table, letting that name settle onto all of them. He then followed his two words with, "He's still out there. I'm pretty sure I know where he is. The police who could check the place out won't do it. They don't believe I know anything about where he is. I want to go get him. And we have enough reason to do it. A signed contract with his wife's immediate family."

"That's good, Roy. The thing is though, you know how tied up everyone of us is right now," Mack said. "It will be difficult for all of us to help at the same time. So I think Lisa and I will be the only ones who can help you take him right now."

"That's okay, Mack," he answered. "I'm not asking for help. I just want everyone's okay on this. Wanda and I can take him. I don't think he'll be anywhere near the problem everyone else thinks he will."

"He's already killed a lot of people," Lisa said, disagreeing with Roy. "That make's him especially dangerous. He'll be desperate if he's cornered. He won't hesitate to kill either one or both of you."

The only heads at the table that didn't shake in agreement with Lisa were Roy, Wanda, and Mack.

Mack explained what he was thinking about Roy's idea. "I think it would be a good idea for Lisa and I to go with you when you go after Savage. But I also am fairly sure that you can bring him in without us. I don't, however, think there's much chance you'll be able to do it with him still alive. It's very unlikely that he'll be willing to surrender. So the question is, are you two prepared for that?"

"We have to be," Wanda answered for Roy. "If we aren't, I don't think we should continue doing private detective work. As much as I don't like the idea of killing anyone, there will be times. So the answer is yes."

"Good answer," Mack said. "You have a go ahead with your plan from me."

"I guess, from me too," Lisa agreed.

All Roy and Wanda got from everyone else was positive nods. But that was all they needed. They were set to drive north as soon as breakfast was done.

Paul decided that it was time to tell everyone about what he saw when he checked out the drug companies building, suspected of holding large numbers of dogs and cats. He told them what it looked like, then about the small building on the other side of the road.

"And parked in front of that building," he said, ending his description, "a brown, Ford cargo van was parked. It had a large dent over the right rear wheel."

"That does tie a lot together," Mack said. "The van used in the observed dead animal dumping. The comment the banker made about borrowing money to a research facility. And the fact that the banker reacted when you mentioned the Ford van."

Paul looked at Sue. "Now we have to see what more we can learn about the banker and Jabber Research."

"I'll get on it right after breakfast," Sue said. "But now, I have something to discuss with all of you. It's personal, but it could have an effect on what we do somewhere down the line. Dale asked me out. On a dinner date. The kind you dress up for."

Lisa's eyes lit up and the expression on her face said, "How wonderful." A sense of relief flooded her. She could now stop feeling responsible for trying to help him through his breakup with Kathy. The invite Sue got to go out for dinner put it all on her shoulders.

Mack was happy to see that Dale was already trying to bring his life back to normal. But he was even happier with the look Lisa had in her eyes and on her face. She was genuinely happy that Dale was interested Sue. It told him something he now felt small for not being sure of from the start. Lisa's motives with Dale truly were only concern about a friend's well being. He would have smiled, if he didn't feel like such a damn fool.

Sue had more to say about it though. She looked at Mack until their eyes met, then said, "Dale also wants you and Lisa to double with us. He said he would feel better about what was going on if you guys were with us." Sue paused, trying to hold back her smile. She shook her head to hold back her laughter. "This date we might be having, is kind of reminding me of my high school years." She paused again, taking a deep breath. "But it could be serious if it ever developed into more than just a date, given our current relationship with him."

"As far as what it might develop into," Mack told her, "that is your personal business. It's none of ours. It just plain isn't right for us to tell you what you can or cannot do in your private life." He smiled, glad he could say what he had to say, and mean it. "And as far as us going out with you and Dale on a formal date, if it's okay with Lisa, it is damn sure okay with me."

Lisa's answer was short. "We are going."

"That's great," Sue said. "I'll call Dale and we'll set up a time."

The conversation at the table went back then, to how to deal with the dead animal investigation. Roy and Wanda were quiet during it though. Lost in their own thoughts about Savage Strange. The big question being, was he in fact at that isolated cabin. If he was, how were they going to take him.

Roy finished eating and went home to get ready to go before anyone else, other than Wanda, was even close to finishing. She finished about five minutes behind Roy. She was nervous, and a little bit scared about what they were facing. But she was anxious too, to get a vicious criminal off the streets and locked up where he could do no more harm.

CHAPTER 15

Savage Strange was about as tired of doing nothing in the cabin but sit around, as he could be of anything. There was absolutely nothing to do. There was no electricity, so there was no decent light to read by. But that didn't matter. His reading skills weren't good enough to get him through a book. Not one beyond a child's picture book that is.

It didn't matter. There were no books to read, even if he could. His cell phone's battery was too low now, to use for anything but making a phone call. That also didn't matter. Making a phone call was advanced as he'd ever gotten with the use of the phone.

He was now reaching the stage that it going out, maybe to the casino, made some sense. After all, what was the point of being free, if you were living like you were in jail. And here in this cabin was worse than jail. At least in jail, he'd have other convicts to talk to. Here, there was no one other than the babbling fool tied up on the floor, whining that his hand and his feet hurt.

If he didn't stop his crying and complaining soon, Savage knew he would be forced to shoot the man one more time. And this time, it would stop his bitching. A bullet to the head was always all the persuasion needed.

The thoughts of killing his hostage cheered him up so much, that Savage decided to go out for a while. The casino would be his first stop this time. He needed the action more than he needed anything else.

Just before he left the cabin, he told his prisoner, "I'm going out for a while. I want you to be a good boy while I'm gone." He laughed at his own perverted humor on his way to his car. He was still smiling when he went inside the casino.

People around him, however, weren't smiling. After being isolated the way he was, he'd forgotten how he looked. And because it was part of him, he grown accustomed to the way he smelled. Which was decidedly unpleasant. He was so happy to be there though, that he didn't notice the way everyone who came near him quickly moved away. It wasn't until he won his first hand of blackjack that he noticed how they backed away from him.

"What the hell?" he thought, before he realized why they were doing what they were doing. It really irritated him. After the isolation of the cabin, when he was finally out among people, he was still isolated.

He left the table and went into the restroom. He cleaned himself up the best he could, then went back to his gambling. The strange thing then was the fact that he won more than he lost.

It was something that rarely happened to him, so he hated to quit when he did. But knew he had no choice. He'd already stayed longer than he should have. Staying any longer, and his chances of being recognized and caught were too great.

He played three more hands anyway. He won the first one, then lost the next two. The loses didn't bother him too much. He was betting against the odds on both, so they were on the conservative side.

After leaving the casino, he felt better with his gambling fever settled down some. He was an addicted gambler, but was able to stop when he had to. He didn't always need to lose all his money first.

This time, he managed to stop while he was ahead. With enough money to go shopping and still have some left over. His first stop was to the discount center. He went to the men's department and picked out a complete change of clothes. What he was wearing was grubby enough to make him anxious to get fresh clothes on. He was wearing them when he went to the grocery department. This was where he planned to spend, what was for him, some serious money.

From there, he knew it would definitely be time to get back to the cabin. Right now, he was sure it was the only truly safe place for him. But what lay ahead for him said otherwise. It was no longer a safe place for him.

Roy and Wanda had already parked their pickup out of sight of the driveway leading to Savage's cabin, and from the cabin itself. The condition of the gravel driveway, now covered with grass, indicated that it was used recently. There was no vehicle parked near the cabin though. That concerned them. Did the lack of a vehicle mean that Savage had been there, but was now gone? Or was he just out somewhere and planning to come back.

They decided that one of them should go inside and look around. The condition of the inside might yield enough clues to answer their question. They decided that Wanda should be the one to do it. Although he would never admit it, when Roy worked with Wanda, he always tried to put her in the least vulnerable situations. It eased his guilt some, for letting her be involved with what was often dangerous work.

Wanda, on the other hand, liked the dangerous parts of detective work. And since she considered going inside to be more dangerous than staying outside, she delighted in being the one doing it.

What she saw when she got there was a surprise though. They'd expected that Savage would either kill him shortly after taking him captive, or at least keep the man with him at all times.

Wanda's first look at the man was one of curiosity. From the way he was tied, it appeared to her that he could have escaped if he'd put enough effort into it. So why didn't he? She bent down to untie him, and asked, "Why the hell are you just laying here? You could have escaped if you tried."

"I can't walk. Look at my feet. He shot me."

As soon as she looked at them, she could see his problem. Now that she knew why he wasn't doing anything to help himself, she asked him about Savage. "Do you know where Savage is? Is he coming back?"

"I don't know where he is. He didn't say where he was going. But he did say he was coming back."

"I don't supposed he said when, did he?"

Wanda was having a hard time showing Harold Cramer much, if any, sympathy. Bullet wounds in his hand and feet or not. She considered him to be part idiot and part extremely ignorant. Using his gun in that crowded store the way he did was enough for her to lose any respect for him she might have otherwise had. Killing a three year old child because he was such a terrible shot with the gun he fired was way too much for her.

As far as she was concerned, there was no excuse for it. She had an ability with guns that went far beyond what most people could ever obtain. No matter how hard they worked at it. Yet she never would have made the same shot he did. It simply was too dangerous, given the crowd that was there.

So she asked him, "What the hell ever possessed you to shoot and kill that little girl? What you did was as about as stupid a move as a person could possibly make."

"No, it wasn't. It was the only move I could make. I had to stop him. It would have been wrong to just let him go. It was my duty to do what I could do to stop him."

"You're duty? To shoot into a crowd of people? When you obviously don't have the ability to shoot it accurately? You go way beyond ordinary stupidity. I hope you know that."

"You're wrong. I've been trained in the use of weapons, and when to use them. The group I belong to believes that it's a persons responsibility to get involved an incident like that. Even if there is collateral damage."

"Collateral damage?" Wanda's voice dripped with sarcasm now. She suspected that he was what he was. And it wasn't something she had the slightest respect for. "That's a military term. You think you're some kind of soldier?" She was somewhat less than gentle as she continued to untie him.

He gave her an, I am a superior look, as a smirk spread across his face. "We…every member of our regiment, is a soldier for Christ. It is our duty to use every means possible to stop anyone going against his teachings. It doesn't matter if what we do affects someone else. Jesus wants us to be involved. Just as he wants us to put a stop to everything the Godless liberals do."

"You believe then, that Jesus wanted you to kill that innocent child?"

"Of course he did. The child was needed in heaven. All I did was deliver her to him. It was, really, the righteous thing to do."

Wanda didn't bother asking anymore questions. This person who killed an innocent little girl, was never going to understand anything she had to say. He was too far into his chosen brainwashing to ever understand what really mattered. He was an excellent reminder of why Mack, Ben, and Roy, held men like him in such total contempt. They were not only stupid. As far as anything positive, they were totally useless. The same as most men who belonged to a paramilitary group.

She helped Harold up onto the cot. "Now," she told him, "When he comes back, I want you to keep quiet. You so much as make a sound, there's a good chance that you too, could end up as collateral damage." She couldn't help but snicker when she used the word collateral on him.

She sat down to wait for Savage then. On the cot, as far from Harold as she could. She didn't have to wait long before she heard a car drive up and stop close to the cabin's door.

She immediately heard Roy call out from somewhere close by. "Stand where you are," he yelled, "and put your hands in the air."

A shot rang out, followed by the sound of broken glass. Wanda was sure then, that Roy was the one who fired, given that she heard the glass. A second shot was fired. It was quickly follow by the sound of breaking wood. Savage Strange burst through the door and into the cabin.

Wanda had her favorite automatic in her hand. "Drop your gun and get face down on the floor," she demanded.

He didn't see her right away, but he did recognize her voice as being one that belonged to a woman. He didn't believe she could shoot him. She would be too weak. Women were always weak. He'd beaten the hell out of plenty of them in his life, so he damn well did know how weak they were.

He dropped to the floor, rolling toward one side of the room. He stopped, lying on his stomach, with both hands holding his gun. He fired wildly in Wanda's direction.

Her first instinct was to duck for cover. She overcame it. She stood upright, took about three seconds to steady her hands and arms, then rapidly pumped three shots directly between his eyes. Looking at the hole her bullets made, they were in such a tight formation that it was difficult to tell that he was shot more than once.

She turned to Harold, who was shaking from fear. His eyes were locked open wide, amazed at what she'd just done. She gave him a grim look. "You saw what I just did with my gun. You now know what I can do with one. But even I would never have fired into that crowd the way you did. I'm going to recommend to the cops when they get here, that you be locked up for murdering that little girl."

Roy ran into the cabin. "Are you okay, Wanda?"

"I'm fine Roy. But I had to shoot the monster on the floor."

Roy looked over at Savage's body. "I heard three shots. How could you miss him twice?"

"I didn't."

Roy looked a second time. "My god," he said, "that's hard to believe, even for me. And I know how good a shot you are."

"Well," Wanda answered, "I took a couple of extra seconds to aim. I knew he wasn't that much better with a gun than Harold here."

For the first time, Roy looked over at him. Like Wanda, he had a difficult time having any sympathy for the man. Harold didn't return Roy's looks. He knew now, that being a soldier for Christ or not, he'd never get so much as an inkling of respect from either of the people in the cabin with him. And after seeing Wanda shoot, he knew he didn't deserve any.

Roy called the state police then. He told them where they were, and the fact that Savage Strange was there too. He also told them that he'd been shot.

"You mean to tell me that you and your wife shot and arrested, on your own, a man who is guilty of multiple murders. I find that very hard to believe. I'm more inclined to believe that you've just cooked up some publicity scheme."

"Not hardly. Have you got a cell phone? Because if you have, I will send you pictures of him to you. I can also send you a picture of the hostage he was holding."

"You'd better be telling the truth," the cop stated firmly. "Or else you will be in a lot of trouble."

Roy got the man's number. He took some pictures with his own cell phone, then texted them to the cop. He quickly responded to Roy.

"Okay, now I believe you. It appears though, on the photos you sent, that Strange is dead."

"That he is. He fired at my wife. She retuned it. When you get here and check the crime scene, you'll see what happened. Not to mention that we have a witness."

The state police came then, bringing the FBI along with them. The crime scene people verified what Roy and Wanda told them. But every person in law enforcement who was a there had the same question. "Who really did the shooting? And why were they lying about it?"

Wanda finally took them outside to a spot it was safe to shoot. When she finished demonstrating her ability with her gun, hitting vey kind of target they could dream up, they believed her.

It was so late by the time they finished with the police, they decided to stay the night in a motel. As she lay in the hard mattress, trying to go to sleep, she couldn't help but wonder. Who of the two men she dealt with that day was the worst. The multi murderer? Or the soldier for Christ? Either way though, it was a chinch that neither one of them had ever had anything positive to offer the world.

CHAPTER 16

That same night, Mack and Lisa were already asleep when his cell phone went off. He was groggy when he rolled over on his side and reached for the, what seemed to him at the time, screaming monster. He fumbled with it for a moment, then brought it up to his ear.

"Yeah, what?" was his answer.

"Are you Mack?" a soft, feminine voice asked.

"It is."

"Thank God," He heard what sounded like a choking sob, follow by, "I know it's late and I have no business calling you. This is Kathy. I need to talk to someone. And I would like it to be you."

"I can appreciate that you want to talk, Kathy. But why me. It's not like we've ever been particularly close since you and Dale got married. Friendly, yes, but not close."

"I know we haven't. And for that, I'm sorry. I've been too busy chasing a dream to pay the attention I should have to what really matters."

"That still doesn't tell me why you called me."

"I just need to talk to someone. Someone I can trust. I think I can trust you."

"Really? And why is that?"

"My mother. She trusted you, Mack. She never explained to me why you and her were what you were. But she was firm about it when she said she trusted you."

Her comments about her mother brought a hoard of memories flooding through Mack's head. He and her mother, Linda, were lovers and soulmates of a sort for some time before she was murdered. They were closer than all but a few couples ever get to be .It hadn't mattered that she was nearly twenty years older than Mack. Nor had it mattered that her husband, Kathy's father, knew of the affair. He never objected to it. Only death parted them. So Mack at least somewhat understood why Kathy called him. But the reason for the call left him lost. From his point of view, if she wanted to change something in her life, Dale was the one she should have called.

"I don't know that there's anything I can say or do that could possibly help you, Kathy. But I will listen to whatever what you want to tell me."

"I hoped you would, Mack." She paused, crying softly. "I…I've really screwed up my life. Our lives. Mine and Dale's. What I did, when I told him I wanted a divorce, was stupid. I was so wrong. I am so damn sorry for doing it. For what else I've done. But I don't know what to do."

"That's not hard to figure out, Kathy. If you want to save your marriage. If you really do care enough about him to make it worth saving, you have to call him. Maybe cancel part of you tour and go home. As far as I'm concerned, fixing what you broke is worth whatever that might cost you. Including any amount of money. I appreciate you wanting to talk to me, but you two are the ones who need to work together to do it."

"I know. And you are right about the money. It isn't worth much right now. But I've been so wrong. I'm afraid to face him. I think he might hate me when I tell him. I cheated on him, Mack. I didn't want to, but when it happened, I didn't stop it. I knew I should but I didn't. I just let him finish what he started. Dale's going to hate me for that."

"Not if you don't tell him. Sometimes that's he best way to deal with it."

"I can't do that. I can't lie to him. Keeping it a secret will be just another lie. I just love him too much to treat him that way."

Mack sighed in frustration at her last comment. He knew he would sound harsh when he asked her, but he had to ask. "If you love him so much, then why the hell did you ask for a divorce?"

"I don't really know. When I did it, I guess I thought it would be better than the way we were living at the time. With me gone so much, either learning new material, in the recording studio, or on the road for long periods of time, it seemed like it wasn't working."

"You should have tried talking to someone then. Anyone of us would have told you how much he loved you. Enough, Kathy, so he was willing to wait on the sidelines for you to have the career you wanted. He would have been there for you when it was over."

"I realize that now. And I know how totally stupid I was. I knew I was wrong when I finished the first concert. When it was over, all I wanted to do was call him. We always talked after a concert. When I couldn't, I was devastated."

"Well, I guess I can understand that. But you did have your new lover there, didn't you? Wasn't he the support you expected?"

"No, he definitely wasn't. And after he did what I didn't stop him from doing, I told him I didn't want him to ever come near me again."

"Who was he, that he was on tour with you?"

"The head of the road crew."

"So he's still with you?"

"No, he is not. Because of his behavior, I fired him. I hope to never see him again."

"Well, that is the best thing you could have done, if you want to fix things with Dale. But you will, one way or the other, have to talk to him if it's going to happen."

"I'll try. But I'm so scared I've screwed things up so bad they can't be fixed. I was so totally damn stupid. So wrong. I guess I don't have much hope for us. Do you think though, that when I go home again, the rest of you will be able to forgive me for what I did to him."

"Of course we will. And so will Dale, whether you and he reconcile or not. We all know that you have a good heart. There aren't any of us who are perfect. Like it or not, we all need forgiveness at times."

"Thank you for talking to me, Mack. And no matter what happens with me and Dale. Or with anything else as far as that goes. I would very much like it if, when I come home, you would be my friend. I would like, someday, to walk in that refuge of yours, holding your hand while you tell me all about it."

"When you come home, Kathy, I would be proud to do that with you."

"I'm glad. You take care now. And tell that beautiful, perfect wife of yours, that I said hi." She hung up.

Lisa, who was silent but awake through Mack's entire conversation with Kathy, said. "Now that was a phone call I never would have expected. Who would have thought Kathy would be calling you?"

"No one, least of all me. And I sure wouldn't have expected her to call me because she wanted to talk to someone about her and Dale."

"She wants to stop the divorce and go back to him, doesn't she?"

"She does."

"Why doesn't she just do it then?"

"She doesn't think he'll be willing to do it, Lisa. She cheated on him, and insists she has to tell him. If she does, he might not take her back."

"I don't know that telling him about the cheating is the right thing or the wrong thing to do. But carrying something like that around for the rest of your life could turn into a heavy burden."

"It could, And if she doesn't tell him, there's always a chance he could find out some other way."

"So what do you think she's going to do, Mack?"

"I wish I knew. But for now, It's time to go back to bed. We do need to get some sleep tonight."

Lisa agreed. Then, when they were both in bed and he was snuggled close to her back, she started to think about what separating would be like. She shivered, and pushed her self against him. Her movements had an immediate effect on him.

She smiled to herself, twisted around to face him, and said, "I love you, Mack Thomas, and sleep isn't what I need or want right now." She moved on top of him. Using her hand as a guide, she brought a smile to his face too.

CHAPTER 17

Breakfast in the morning started different from what was normal. Mack and Lisa were late, but they beat Roy and Wanda there anyway. Stranger then that, Lisa's sister, Julie, made the first comment when Mack and Lisa sat down at the table.

"Why is it, Lisa," she asked, "that you can come here looking so tired, yet still have that smile on your face? You have kind of a glow or something about you too."

Lisa looked at her younger sister. She lightly shook her head. Julie was, in Lisa's opinion, too young to be asking questions like that. So she wasn't at all sure how she should answer it. Then Wanda and Roy arrived, and she avoided the answer.

"You're late," Mack said the moment they walked in. He did it, only because that's the kind of thing Roy was fond of doing to him. Especially since he married Lisa and was late so often.

"Well, given the lives you all lead," Ben said, "it's a wonder you aren't late more often. Do any of you four late comers want anything special, or should I make your usual breakfast?"

Wanda answered him. "I love my usual breakfast," she said, "but this morning, after yesterday, I need something sweet. Just to get the evil taste out of my mouth."

"No problem," Ben agreed with the request. "But why the evil taste? Was yesterday that bad?"

"It was both good and bad," Roy answered. "We got Savage Strange, but Wanda was forced to shoot him to do it. So that was both bad and good. Almost as bad, she had to spend some time, too much time, with Strange's hostage. That moron, Harold Cramer."

"He was the one who shot the kid, wasn't he," Lisa commented.

"He was," Wanda answered. "Savage had already shot him three times since he took him hostage. In one hand and both feet. It was hard though, to feel any sympathy for him. He was such a total ass. When I asked him about shooting and killing that poor little kid, he thought he had a good excuse for doing it."

Paul, who was silent until he heard about the man having an excuse for what he did, asked the question they all wanted an answer to. "How could he possibly have any excuse for what he did?"

Wanda explained about the man being a soldier for Christ, and how the girl was just collateral damage. And how she was needed in heaven. "And he," Wanda explained, "was full of a lot of other religious bullshit."

Julie spoke up then. "I don't think you should call anything that is religious, what you just called what he said."

"I only did it, Julie, because the word bullshit best describes what came out of his mouth. The truth is, nothing he said was religious. For him, and for all those people who belong to those paramilitary groups, religion is just something to give them an excuse to commit atrocities."

"Putting religion aside for the moment," Paul interrupted them. He directed a question to Roy. "Are you two going to be able to assist us with our case now? Or do you have other things going."

"We should be able to help some right away. But we will also be cleaning up some easier cases. Hopefully, we'll be available full-time in a couple of days. So what is the status of your case?"

Sue answered this question. "After considerable digging through a ton of files, I've established that Paul's banker acquaintance has authorized loans to Jabber Research. They are definitely are in some way connected to doing business with Davis Drugs. They own the big buildings where the animals are being killed. I also managed to get into the animal control's investigation files. They've autopsied a lot of dead dogs and cats, but they still aren't sure what's killing them. They suspect though, that it's something new. Probably a virus. The thing that worries them the most about what ever it is, is the fact they are pretty sure it can be spread through the air. So it's incredibly dangerous. Especially if it can attack more than dogs and cats."

"Do they, does anyone, have any idea where this virus originated?" Roy asked.

"Not really," Mack said. "But I have an idea about it."

"And that is?"

"I think, Roy, that the Davis Drug company is somehow responsible for it. I don't know if they discovered it or created it. But they're the reason for what's going on."

"But why are they killing so many cats and dogs? It doesn't make any sense."

"We have some ideas on that too," Paul said. "This might sound pretty far out, but it could be possible that they are searching for an antidote to the virus."

"The trouble with that idea," Roy complained, "is that they're obviously spending a lot of money on what they're doing. Pretty much all drug companies, no matter who or what they're making drugs for, only care about profits."

"And if they succeed in what they're trying to do," Mack explained, "they'll be making unbelievable profits."

"How do you figure that?"

"If they can come up with an antidote, a cure, for the virus they've created, the sales of that drug will make them incredible profits. Especially because the virus is so deadly."

"But the virus doesn't seem to be infecting any dogs, other than the ones they are killing."

"It will if they release it." Mack frowned. "And you can damn well believe it, that that is exactly what they plan on doing."

"So," Roy asked, his voice filled with the disgust he felt. "What in the hell can we do about it?"

Sue voiced her opinion on what to do. "Davis Drugs is having a difficult time keeping people working where the dogs and cats are. While researching them, I found out they are constantly hiring. I think that one of the things we need to do is put someone inside. We need to learn more about what they are doing and how they are doing it."

"That sounds like it could be dangerous," Roy said, "So I think it should be one of us men to do it. We've put you women into too much danger lately."

Sue smiled at him. A smile filled with the kind of frustration they all felt. "The trouble with that, Roy, is the fact that they are only hiring women for the job."

"Well, damn, why are they doing that?"

"I think it's because of the mistaken belief that women are always easier to intimidate than men are."

"That's not a problem," Lisa told them. "I've already decided to be the one to go inside. I need more experience doing undercover work anyway."

Roy looked at Mack. "What do you think about her doing that?"

"I hate the idea. But if that's what she thinks she should do, it isn't up to me to try to tell her no. Besides, if needed, she can defend herself as well as any of us."

"The thing is, Roy," Paul explained this time. "We are going to need a second volunteer. We need someone to go undercover at that Jabber Research facility. We really need to know what it is that they are doing for Davis Drugs. We can't go after them the way we want to until we do."

"That's no problem," Wanda said, looking at Roy. "I'll do it. It can't be any worse than what I had to do yesterday. Spending as much time as I did with that Harold Cramer was decidedly unpleasant."

"Damnit," Roy complained, "I hate it when we put you two in dangerous situations like that."

"I can understand that," Lisa said. "But that's a two way street. We hate it when you guys go into a dangerous situation too. So I think you should try to get used to it. Or, at least try to accept it."

"That's right," Wanda added. "Because if you can't, then I think we should shut the agency down. Then we can all go ahead and find something less dangerous to do. Like raise cattle again."

"We know you're both right," Roy conceded. "But it's a far easier thing to say, that it is to do."

CHAPTER 18

Sue created IDs for Lisa and Wanda that gave them the kind of background the drug company and research company would want them to have. They were hired right after they were interviewed. The drug company was especially pleased with Lisa. Not that many people would be as delighted as she was about making twenty-two fifty an hour, just for working where dogs and cats were being experimented with.

Lisa was glad they thought she was excited about her new job. It was difficult, while she was being interviewed, to pretend that she wanted the job, let alone was excited about it.

She started work the next morning. Because she was a new employee, the guards at the gate where she entered the parking lot for the facility, were extra cautious when they checked her company supplied ID.

She wore the company uniform, which was a well used pair of blue coveralls. It fit her loose and sloppy enough to hide her body camera, and had the added benefit of showing almost nothing of her figure. She wasn't wearing any makeup, and her hair was up in a bun. About as ugly a hairdo as she could come up with. It did little though, to eliminate any of the guards constant sexual innuendo while they held her ID far longer than needed.

She needed to get passed another guard before she could get to the time clock and punch in. He stalled her so long it was only one minute before her start time when she punched in. She was sure then, that everyday in that place would be a long one.

The workspace inside the building was one huge room. It was filled with a series of cubicles, with one woman in each cubicle. When they first went into their assigned space, some, who like Lisa didn't already have an assigned animal, were brought one. Two out of three were given dogs. The rest got cats. Lisa got a medium size, mixed breed dog. It was caged, and the cage was placed on the table.

The guard who brought it, reached into the cage and slipped a leash over the dog's neck. He then took the dog out of the cage. He handed the leash to Lisa, then gave her two small, sealed envelopes and a page of instructions. He pointed out everything else already in the cubicle, that she'd need to complete her task.

The last thing he said was, "Be sure to wear the mask hanging over there." He pointed it out. "When you handle either powder. They aren't really dangerous, so the mask is just a safety measure. But be sure to wear it anyway." Without warning, he tried to put his hand over her breast. "And if you need a bathroom break, you'll have to wait for me to come around to cover for you."

Lisa pushed his hand away long before he finished talking. "Don't be doing that crap with me," she warned him. "I really don't like it."

He laughed. "Well, you should know, or you should at least learn, that here it doesn't matter a damn if you do or you don't. The only way you're going to keep working here is if I say you're doing the job properly. That means there's more to what you got to do, then take care of that damn dog."

Lisa watched his back as he left her cubicle. She knew already that she'd be lucky to make it a full day there. That meant she would have to learn as much as possible about the place as she could.

The first thing she needed to do, according to her instructions, was to give the dog some food in a bowl. Before doing so, she was required to pour the meager contents of the envelope specified over the food.

Because she was sure it was the virus inside, there was no way she was about to give it to the dog. So she tucked the envelope into the far reaches of her coveralls. It not only would save the dog's life for a while, it would screw up their testing. If they believed he got the virus, and he was healthy later, they would think the new antidote worked. As instructed, she let the dog eat, then took his temperature. She also looked into his mouth and noted the color of his tongue. It was supposed to turn a sick yellow. The last thing she watched for was heavy drooling. All symptoms she recorded as the dog having,

She followed the instructed routine every forty-five minutes. The guard came around almost that frequently. And every time he did, he tried to make some kind of move on her. Each time, she managed to push him off. She also recorded his actions.

She then finally reached the point whee she had no choice but to use the restroom. She called the guard over so he could watch the dog. That was something he had absolutely no intention of doing. As soon as she was out of the cubicle, he tied the dog's leash to a hook on the side of the table and followed Lisa.

She was using a stall in the room when he came in there. He waited until she finished, but was standing there with a broad grin on his face when she came out. Lisa knew then that she wasn't going to be able to just walk away this time. She turned on the camera.

"I know," she said, her voice grim, "that you think that you can do whatever it is you want to do to me now. The thing is though, you can't. If you are at all smart, you will turn around and walk out of here right now. Because if you don't, and you try to make a move on me, I will hurt you. And the mood I'm in now, I will hurt you bad."

He laughed so hard he almost choked on it. "Sure," he bragged, "a pretty little girl like you is going to hurt a grown man like me. Not hardly. I'm a trained fighter. There just ain't many men I can't beat. Knocking you into shape is going to be easy. So the smart thing for you to do is strip down now. It'll save a lot of hassle. Because no matter what, I am going to have you today. You are just too damn good looking to miss this chance."

"That's not going to happen."

He shook his head. It aggravated him that she wasn't smart enough to just let him have his due. He moved to grab her, expecting her to give in as soon as he had his hands on her. Of course she didn't. First because he never got his hands on her. Second, because whether he did or didn't get his hands on her, she was going to retaliate. And she was going to do it in a way he would never forget.

Before he could even begin to comprehend what she was doing, she got a hold of the thumb on his right hand. With a quick twist, she broke it. As soon as he tried pulling his thumb away. She held on, separating the break. Another twist, and part of the bone was poking through his skin. It was bleeding. When he grabbed his broken thumb with his other hand, she poked him in his eyes. It was just hard enough to bring on a deluge of tears, temporarily blinding him. She didn't permanently blind him. Although she was tempted.

She stepped back now, appreciating the fact that she'd rendered him helpless to defend himself. She had no desire though, to show him any mercy. As good a person as she otherwise was, she would never forget when she was kidnapped and raped by so many men so many times. At the time it was happening, the number of men doing it seemed endless. She eventually recovered from the physical pain. The pain they inflicted on a special place inside her brain, was never going to leave her.

This man in front of her, trying to regain his sight while he was also trying to ease the pain in his broken thumb, was just another of those vicious, more than useless creatures. That meant he had a special place inside her. With every bit of strength she had in her body, she reared back and kicked him between the legs. He screamed in pain and dropped to his knees, both hands now holding tightly to the latest source of pain. Blood from his thumb coated the front of his pants.

Looking at him, she said, "Are you satisfied with what you're going to do to me yet? Why aren't beating the hell out of me while you're raping me?"

He groaned, "I'm going to kill you, you fucking bitch."

"Really? Right now? You're a fighter. Get off your knees and kill me. You chicken shit piece of nothing."

He tried to stand but fell back on his knees. "I swear. I will kill you."

"Maybe." She knew then that she'd wasted enough time with him. It was time to get back to her cubicle and the dog she hadn't put to death with their killing powder. "Remember," she reminded him, "that I said I would hurt you bad if you didn't stop?"

"I'll kill you, bitch." This time his voice and a lot less bluster to it.

Lisa didn't care what his voice had though. Or anything else about him. She kept her promise to him. She hurt him by kicking him under the chin. Not hard enough to break his neck and kill him. But hard enough so that he would be screwed up for a very long time. Probably screwed up enough to keep him from committing any rapes. She left him sprawled on the restroom floor. Unconscious.

She went back to her cubicle and spent the rest of the afternoon faking what she was supposed to be doing. All the time expecting to be thrown out of the building for beating up the guard.

The second sealed envelope she was given contained what the company hoped was an antidote that worked. She hid that, along with the killing powder, in her coveralls. She knew that both packets of powder would tell them a lot when they were analyzed later.

She expected that whether not her rapist guard regained consciousness, someone would find him. She was sure too, that when he was found, they would figure out it was her that did him in.

But it didn't happen. Although all of the women working there used the restroom that afternoon, none of them said anything to anyone about the guard on the floor. In fact though, a few of them who walked passed her cubicle on their return from the restroom, softly said things like, "Nice. Good job. I hope you stay. and About time."

He was still there, still unconscious, when the second shift arrived. They would watch the animals until midnight. At that time, the ones who hadn't died were again caged and moved to the animal's night room.

The person who relieved Lisa commented on the condition of her dog. "He looks better than any of the dogs I've worked with so far," she said. "Did you give him all the stuff this morning?"

"Oh, yes," Lisa assured her. "I did everything according to the instructions. I didn't want to mess up. I need this job. It pays better than any job I've ever gotten before."

"Well good. Maybe they've finally found what they've been looking for. Trouble with that is though, if they have, most of us will be laid off."

"That wouldn't be so good for me."

"Me either. As much as I hate seeing all these dogs and cats die, I really need the money too."

Knowing she couldn't keep up her charade with the woman, Lisa left. As she was going out the door, she heard a woman scream inside. Trying to act as if she didn't hear anything, she continued to the pickup she was driving.

By the time she reached the gate to exit, the guards there had gotten the news about the injured guard inside the building. Since they didn't know what caused the problem yet, they didn't try to stop her. But she was only two minute away when they did lock the place down.

The women from the first shift, who were still there after the scream, were interrogated for two hours before they were allowed to leave. The guard was carried away by ambulance. He was first taken to the emergency room. From there it was intensive care. It was there that he was told it would take at least several months, if not a few years. of therapy before he could walk on his own again. Normal sex for him in the future was an unknown.

The only thing he could think about, once he was given enough pain killers to think, was how he was going to find Lisa and get even with her. He didn't know it, but he'd never be able to find her. The ID Sue created for her when she applied for the job would make it an impossible thing to do.

That fact gave Lisa confidence, once she was out of the Davis Drug parking lot, that it was very unlikely she would ever have to worry about repercussions from either Davis Drug or the security guard. That left her feeling good about what she'd accomplished during her single day under cover at Davis Drug.

Mack, and everyone else at Refuge Rescuers, agreed with her.

CHAPTER 19

Wanda's first day at Jabber Research was far less eventful than Lisa's first day at the Davis Drug facility. She got through the day without any problems, and satisfied her employers with her ability to grasp the skills needed to do her job quickly. She learned that they were definitely trying to develop an antidote for a virus that affected dogs and cats. She also learned that it was a task that was proving to be very difficult for them to do. She stayed with the job for three days. Three times as long as Lisa stayed with hers. But then, she didn't beat up any armed guards either.

They continued then, to learn as much more about what Davis Drug was doing. It was tedious work, and they were all somewhat frustrated with it. So they decided to take a break from it for the weekend.

For Mack and Lisa, it was a much needed time to relax. Especially with the upcoming date for dinner with Dale and Sue. It was something they were both looking forward to and, at the same time, dreading.

It would be Dale's first outing since he had dinner with Lisa, Sue, and Mack, right after Kathy asked for the divorce. And that time was mostly Lisa's idea. An idea that had proved less positive than she hoped it would be. Completely unexpected to her, Mack got upset about the arrangement. It seemed so out of character for him.

This time, taking Sue out to dinner was Dale's own idea. He hadn't been apart from Kathy, with a divorce hanging over his head, all that long. They were somewhat concerned about how he would handle it. They knew, no matter what he said, that he wasn't over Kathy yet. And he wouldn't be for a very long time.

At the same time, they were happy that he was willing to try to start living a normal life again. And in the long term, there were some things in his life that would improve if he could get over Kathy.

If he could find another woman to love and to share his life with, it was much more likely that she would be there for him than Kathy ever would or could be. She had her singing career, and that always came first. Dale was second. Dale loved her enough to deal with it, but it did make their relationship a lot more difficult than what it otherwise would be.

At the same time Mack and Lisa were having those thoughts, so was Kathy. She'd just finished another more than simply successful concert. Her fans, who were lucky enough to be there, were thrilled with her performance. She sang for them longer that night, then she had ever done. And the standing ovation she received at the end was but one of three she received that night.

She should have been filled with joy, and totally satisfied with her life when she went to her dressing room. Instead, she locked her door. Remembering the phone call she used to make, she fell on the bed, crying her heart out. Not having Dale to share her success, left it meaning far less than it did when she could share it with him.

When she finally recovered enough to think about it, about her life, she no longer had any doubts about it. She made a terrible mistake. All the adulation, all the applause, and all the money she was making, weren't worth what she'd so cavalierly thrown away.

She had a followup concert scheduled for the following night. It was Friday now, so she knew the crowd would be to capacity. Even the standing room. She knew that for the sake of her career, it was extremely important that she give as good a performance as any she'd ever done.

Then she realized that she'd done that for a very long time now. Since the beginning of her career. And she'd been successful beyond her wildest dreams. Dreams which now seemed to matter so little. Dreams that if she continued to follow, would leave her a rich, famous, empty shell of a person.

If she was going to change that, she needed to do it now. She had to make the choice. She couldn't just leave things the way they were. No matter how Dale reacted, no matter what he decided, she had to chase the one dream hat mattered the most. And that wasn't on any stage.

She set up her laptop on the small desk in her dressing room and got online. Saturday or not, there had to be a way to fly to Minnesota. If she could, she would rent a car. By sometime Saturday night, she would hopefully be seeing Dale again.

While she was looking forward to seeing Dale, he was looking forward to spending an evening with friends. He wasn't a close friend to Sue, but they did know each other well enough to know they liked each other. As far as a romantic involvement was concerned though, Sue was doubtful it would occur between her and Dale. She could see dating him, and the possibility of that leading them into bed was something she might eventually consider. But nothing permanent.

Sue, Dale knew, would be who he focused on during the evening. But he was looking forward too, to seeing Mack and Lisa. They were his best friends. And because they were all in law enforcement, they would have no problems with carrying on a conversation.

Dale picked up Sue that evening. He was driving Kathy's car. He wasn't sure if using it would upset her or not, but the way he was feeling at the time, it didn't really concern him. It was a far better vehicle to drive it for something like this, then his pickup or patrol car.

Mack and Lisa went in his pickup. They talked about borrowing someone's car, but decided that their date wasn't so formal that their vehicle mattered.

They met at the restaurant. Dale and Sue were already seated when they got there. They hadn't ordered anything, so they all ordered drinks for the first time when the waitress came around with their menus.

Dale ordered a bourbon on the rocks and Sue and Lisa ordered wine. Mack smiled when he ordered a glass of beer. "So, I'm still a hick country boy. But beer's my favorite drink."

Sue is the one who answered him. "You are a lot of things Mack. But a hick isn't one of them. What you are, really, is the kind of man we all want to marry. Lisa is damn lucky to have you."

Lisa smiled at her. "You are so right," she agreed. "I consider myself to be about as lucky as a woman could get."

"Mack's a lucky man," Dale said, "to have two such beautiful women feel that way about him."

"You don't have anything to be jealous about, Dale," Lisa said as she reached across the table and touched his arm. "Give them time to find out your status, and you'll have most of the single women in Clayborne County chasing you."

The waitress came with their drinks then, and took their food orders.

"So," Dale asked when she was gone, "what have you guys been working on lately?"

Lisa told him about her day in the employ of Davis Drug. Except the details of her fight with the security guard. When she mentioned it, she toned it down considerably.

After eating a well prepared, delicious meal, they moved to the bar area. A band was just starting up, but they all sat at the table they found, rather than consider any dancing. They ordered a round of drinks, but found the music too loud to carry on a decent conversation.

They were all considering leaving, when the usual macho man, who was absolutely certain he was god's gift, asked Lisa to dance. Dale glared at him. "No!" he told the Romeo.

The guy looked at Dale, then answered, "She ain't with you, so who the hell are you to say no for her?"

"I am the man who told you no. So go sit down or bother someone else."

"Listen. All I did was ask her to dance. You don't have to be so nasty about it."

Mack answered him this time. "The answer is no. She's my wife, so go sit down."

The man finally gave up and sat down. He motioned to Mack and Dale for his friends, but they apparently ignored him. Dale suggested then, that they leave the bar and go to his house. "It's too early," he said, "to call it a night."

Mack was somewhat reluctant to go there. He thought that Dale and Sue would have a better time on their own than they would with him and Lisa. She though, was in favor of spending a little more time with Dale and Sue. So they finished their drinks, left the bar, and met at Dale's.

Sue wisely suggested they put on a pot of coffee, rather than have any more to drink. They all agreed. Lisa and Mack sat in a couple of easy chairs, and Sue sat on one side of the love seat while Dale made the coffee. He was carrying a tray with four mugs of coffee, and cream and sugar when he joined them.

Sue picked the love seat to sit on as a test. She was curious as to whether Dale would sit next to her or not. She was pleased when he did. Mack and Lisa were sipping on their black coffee, and Dale and Sue were adding cream and sugar to theirs, when the front door opened.

Before they could react, Kathy stepped into the house. She was carrying a suitcase, which she set down. Her first look at Mack and Lisa was a pleased one. Shock filled her face when she saw Dale and Sue on the love seat together.

She stared at them for only a moment before picking up her suitcase. "I'm sorry," she said, an inkling of tears forming in her eyes. "I should have called." She spoke then, to Dale. "I'll call you tomorrow, if it's okay? I'd really like to talk to you."

Dale was so shocked from seeing her, that he wasn't able to speak. Lisa saved the moment. "I don't think you should leave. You damn well do need to talk to Dale. Mack and I will leave. Sue can either stay, or ride with us."

"I'm staying," Sue said, her voice firm. "I know that these two have a lot to deal with, but I'm here now. Before I go, I'd like to hear what you've got to say for yourself, Kathy. After what you did to Dale. He in no way deserved that. And you damn well know it."

"I wouldn't be here if I didn't know it, Sue." Kathy swallowed hard, struggling to hold her emotions in check. "I couldn't have been more wrong." She again looked at Dale, trying to catch his eyes with hers. "And if you aren't able to ever forgive me, I will understand. I know saying I'm sorry won't cut it, but that's all I've got. That and asking to be forgiven."

Dale couldn't hold his eyes with hers. He hung his head while he answered her. "I don't see how it matters what we try to do. You'll just go back on your big tour, and have your new, I'm sure wonderful lover. And if we were what is supposed to be together, you'll be with some else most of the time anyway."

"That would never happen again. If you can find it in your heart to give me another chance, there will never be another tour. This current one will be done too. And no other man will ever be allowed to so much as touch me." She paused and came close to a small smile. "I'm sorry, Dale. There will be one exception. Mack Thomas will hold my hand when he takes me for walk in his refuge, and teaches me about it. I think I will sometimes need someone to hold my hand. I would like for it to be Mack. My mother would want that too. She loved him for a lot of reasons. The way he could hold her hand was one of the best ones."

Mack felt a stab of sadness float through him when she mentioned her mother, Linda. She had filled a special place in Mack's heart that before she became part of his life, he didn't know was there. It was a place he now only visited alone, on the dark nights when life's terrors wouldn't let him sleep.

"The last thing in the world that could concern me, Kathy," Dale said, still unsure he wanted this conversation, "is you walking in the refuge with Mack. Holding hands or not. What bothers me is what you said you were going to do once you went on tour. I'm not now, nor will I ever be, willing to have anyone in our lives like that. I love you still, Kathy, but I don't doubt that you've already destroyed the trust I had in you."

Kathy leaned against the wall. She looked at everyone there, one person at a time. "I wish," she explained, "that none of you were here now. But you are, so I can't stop you from listening to what I'm going to say. I have no choice but to tell the truth." Her tears flowed freely, and she tried to wipe them away. "I know now that what I'm going to tell you, Dale, will make it impossible to fix what I've so badly broken. You're right. I did cheat on you. Once. Only once. It was close to the worst experience of my life. Since you don't want me to be your wife any longer, it will be a very long time before I'll ever want to do anything like that again. With anyone. You are the only man I want now. Or probably ever will want."

Dale couldn't answer her. He found that what she told him was beyond anything he could ever deal with. Kathy made no effort to hide her tears now. She picked up her suitcase to go.

"Unless I hear from you, Dale, I'll only be here for one day. You still have my cell phone number. I haven't changed it. If you change your mind and are willing to give me another chance, the tour is over. Life, I promise, will be different for both of us."

Kathy set her suitcase back down. She turned to Sue first. "If you are the one who replaces me," she said, hugging her. "You take good care of him. You'll never find a better man."

"You've always been a good friend to all of us, Lisa," she said as she gave her a hug too. "And you keep on taken care of your man. He's the kind of person we should all try to live up to."

"You take care to, Kathy. And call us now and then, so we know how life is treating you."

Kathy then turned to Mack. "Someday," she said, putting her arms around his neck, "Maybe you can tell me about you and mom. But there's something you can do for me tomorrow that's almost as important. Take me for a walk in your refuge. Tomorrow I will need someone to hold my hand."

Mack turned to Lisa for the answer. "Okay?"

"More than okay, Mack. I held Dale's hand when he needed it. There's no reason for you not to hold Kathy's hand when she needs it."

One more time, Kathy picked up her suitcase. Then, before turning away, she wrapped her free hand around the back of Mack's neck, and pulled his head down to meet hers. The kiss goodby that she gave him was all the thank you he would ever need from her.

It was a silent bunch who watched her close the door behind her. They stood there a moment after she was gone. Mack then took Dale's hand and shook it. He gave Sue a kiss on the cheek, then opened the door. Lisa, having already kissed Dale and Sue goodnight, followed him out.

Their ride home was silent, filled with a sense of loss. They showered separately before bed. Once there, she pulled Mack tight to her and held on.

"I don't want to make love tonight," she told him. "Life right now is too damn sad for that. But I do need you to hold me. And maybe never, ever, let me go. I love you, Mack. Please, don't ever let us go where those two are right now."

CHAPTER 20

Kathy spent a restless night. She was sure when she left the house that was once her home, that her marriage was over. Dale would never forgive her for her foolish mistake. She didn't blame him at all. She was the one to blame. And now she would have to live with it. Something that was going to be extremely difficult. Especially since she considered that the biggest and best part of her life was over.

Before doing anything, she tried to decide what to do with her day. Getting out of Kingsburg as soon as possible was on the top of her list. She checked online for a flight that would take her back to the city where she left her crew, but there were no direct flights. She hadn't actually expected that there would be, but was disappointed anyway.

She then went through the hassle of finding the series of flights she would need to take her to the city where her next concert would take place. She booked the tickets for the next day.

She then dragged herself into the shower. She hoped, as she turned the water on, that it and a lot of soap would wash away the crawling dread she felt. Both inside and out. It didn't help. After a thorough scrubbing, then toweling dry, she still felt as dirty as she did the night she let Terrance use her for his satisfaction.

She shivered as she asked herself, one more time, why she didn't stop him. There might have been at least some chance with Dale, if she'd just done that. When she faced the truth, she knew why she didn't. What he did to her was the punishment she thought she deserved after what she did to Dale.

She dressed slowly. A pair of blue jeans, a light blue blouse that went okay with her flaming red hair, and tennis shoes. She knew that good boots would be better for her walk in the refuge with Mack, but she didn't have any with her. And the fact that there would soon be stores open where she could buy a pair didn't at the moment seem relevant. She'd make do with what she had.

She called Mack, to set up a time to meet at the refuge, to start their hike. Lisa answered the phone. Kathy came within a deep breath of hanging up. She didn't feel as if talking to anyone other than Mack, would be any kind of benefit.

Lisa answered with the normal hello, then let Kathy's silence hang in the air for a few moments. She then said, "Kathy, Mack's in the shower. That's why I answered his phone."

Kathy still didn't say anything. She was mentally debating whether or not to go on the hike. It was possible, she was sure, that all of them were disgusted enough with her to not want anything to do with her.

The instant before her finger pushed the button to hangup the phone, Mack came on. "Don't hang up, Kathy. I would very much like it if we could make that walk today. It would be nice, if we could maybe talk about your mom some. It has been way too long since I've been able to do that."

"Okay, Mack," she finally answered. "As long as it doesn't upset Lisa. The last thing I want to do is cause problems for anyone. I've done more than enough of that already. The burden of my troubles belong on my back. No where else."

"Lisa is right here, next to me, Kathy. She's okay with you and I going for a walk today. And just so you know, she wants very much to someday to talk with you about your dad. She considered him to be a close and trusting friend. It was a hard time for her when he died. She did it all at home, but I never saw her cry harder."

"Tell Lisa," Kathy answered, feeling slightly better now that there was something positive she could say, "that as soon as my tour is over, I would love to spend time talking to her about dad."

They set a time then, to meet. Kathy didn't know the refuge very well, so Mack decided on which trail they'd walk. He gave her directions to the trailhead.

They still had enough time, before Mack was going to meet Kathy, to eat breakfast. So they walked to Ben and Theresa's. He was careful to hold Lisa's hand on the way. She gave his hand a light squeeze as they went inside.

Roy saw their somber mood, and knew enough of what they'd been dealing with, to back off his normal teasing. "Good morning," was all he said to them. Wanda nodded her hello and Sue looked at them with blurry eyes. She shook her head slowly from side to side. "Late night," she said.

Ben and Theresa tried to ignore everyone's less than happy faces, and gave Lisa and Mack a cheerful good morning. Ben let his eyes roam over Sue, Mack, and Lisa.

"Tired as you three look," he commented, "it must have been a troubled time last night." He was as concerned about Dale as any of them, so he said, "Did any good come of it."

"No," Sue said flatly. "Kathy came home. It was bad timing. I think she made things worse for them."

"How was Dale doing when you left him last night?" Lisa asked.

"Not good. He's really torn up about what she told him. I don't think he'll ever be able to get passed it. I stayed with him for quite a while, but it didn't seem to help much."

Her words gave Lisa the feeling that she was the one who could help Dale get through it. A feeling she knew would only cause problems if she followed them. They certainly wouldn't solve any. So she wisely kept her mouth shut about them.

"That's too bad," Mack said. "Because regardless of what happened, it wasn't important enough to let it destroy what they had. I think Kathy deserves another chance."

"I'm no so sure about that," Ben said.

"I think Mack's right," Theresa told them. She winked at Mack and smiled. "Mack likes to give people a second chance. That's part of what makes him so special."

Ben looked at his wife. There was a time when Mack gave her a second chance, and he was right in doing it. He knew that, because if Mack hadn't, Theresa wouldn't be his wife. And without her, most of the joy he had in living would be gone.

He knew he needed to correct what he said. "Mack and Theresa are right. She does deserve another chance. We all deserve at least one second chance our lives."

"Now all we have to do is convince both of them of that. She needs to forgive herself as bad as Dale needs to forgive her."

They all agreed about Dale and Kathy, then let the conversation drift on to other things. Mack was mostly silent through the rest of the meal. He was lucky, and everyone avoided pushing him to talk. They knew he was thinking about the day ahead. Which he was. But he was remembering too. There were so many loses in his past. None of which he could change. Now Dale was about to lose in a big way. But in his case he didn't need to. It was one of those perverse things about humans that drove Mack crazy.

And those thoughts filled him with a discomfort about the walk with Kathy he wasn't sure about having. Regardless of the problems she was going through, he wanted their time together to be warm and free of any kind of animosity. Because if there was any, it could easily destroy their ability to talk about Linda. They needed to remember out loud how much she meant to both of them. Mack also genuinely wanted to tell her about the refuge, and the way it was recovering from the devastating fire that burned it just a few years ago. The refuge was about so much of life that mattered to him, and he loved sharing it.

Try as he might to relax, he was a bundle of nerves when he parked at the trailhead. She wasn't there yet, so he opened the window in his pickup, and waited for her inside it. He sipped a cup of still hot, black coffee Ben put in an insulated mug for him.

It was a quiet Sunday morning, so he gradually gained a small sense of peace as he watched what was around him. It was what he thought of as real life taking place in this refuge he loved. It pleased him that the people who would visit there later in the day, were now safely locked away in one church or another. It was as good a place as any to keep them from disturbing the short bit of tranquility he was now enjoying.

He was soon so immersed in what he was experiencing, that he almost missed her when she pulled in and parked. He was a bit flustered when he realized she was there. The last thing he wanted to do is make her feel like he wasn't glad to see her.

When he left his truck to join her, the first sight of her filled him with a sense of wonder. Her clothes fit her perfectly. Not so tight that they looked cheap. It was more that they fit her just the right amount to leave no doubt that her figure was close to perfection. Her beautiful red hair was combed out straight, and flowed just over her shoulders. Her face was free of makeup, and glowed in the bright summer sun. What for Mack completed her incredible beauty, was the freckles sprinkled over her nose.

As he stood in front of her, unable to take his eyes off her, she stared back at him. Her face quickly filled with the look of confusion she felt.

"Is something wrong, Mack?" she asked.

He couldn't help himself. He was embarrassed from the way he looked at her, but her pure beauty so delighted him that he chuckled softly. "There's nothing wrong. It's just that seeing you just now, I was pretty much overwhelmed."

"What are you talking about?" Her voice illustrated her confusion with his unexpected reaction to her. "Is it because of what I told you I did?"

"God no! It's just you. You are unbelievably beautiful, Kathy. I've always thought of you as being very pretty. I was wrong. That's what hit me so hard. You are incredibly, unreal beautiful."

She managed a smile. "It's nice of you to say that. But you don't have to try so hard to make me feel better. Showing me your refuge will be enough for today."

"I'm sorry Kathy, if what I said somehow upsets you. But I only said it because it's true." He stopped to take a deep breath. "I want you to know, if we were in another time and another place, after seeing you the way I'm seeing you now, I would chase you to the ends of the earth to make you mine. And any man who wouldn't do that, is an idiot."

"Even Dale?"

"Mostly Dale. He's my best friend, but if he doesn't get his shit together before you're gone and it's too late, I'll never let him forget what a fool he is."

"You know what, Mack. If this were a different time and a different place, I'd let you catch me. And if it wasn't the fact that I care so much about you and Lisa, and what you have, I would be sorely tempted to take up the ways of my parents. And damn well start something now."

He smiled at her, his eyes telling her he appreciated what she'd just said. He too, if it weren't for Lisa, would accept that life. But he knew what he had, and not even Kathy could convince him to put that in jeopardy.

They held hands as they started down the trail. Every so often, they would squeeze their hands together in a show of affection. They were so intent on each other and their surroundings, that they failed to notice the car that parked in the trailhead parking lot right after they started walking.

Two men, wearing camouflage coveralls, got out of the car. They opened the trunk and took out two rifles in gun cases. Inside them, there were AR15s. Both had mounted scopes and thirty round magazines.

"Time for the bitch to get what she's got coming," Terrance Withers said to the man with him.

Claude Glut, the somewhat chubby little man with Terrance, nodded in agreement. "You damn right," he agreed. "Ain't neither one of us deserved to be fired the way she done it. My group what I belong to now, The Pride Guys, figures bitches like her ain't got no business no how, makin' the kind a money what she does. Kill 'em all, I say."

"You are right. She ain't worth nothin'. I had a piece of her. She was a lousy fuck. But after we kill that cowboy she was holding hands with, I'm going to do her again. Just to let her know I can, before I kill her."

"You can kill her. I don't care which one of us does that. But you ain't gonna do it until I get a taste of her too. Lousy fuck or not, there ain't no way I can pass by something what looks that good, without having a piece of it."

"You'll get your chance. But we'd best get moving, if we're going to finish them before the whole damn day disappears."

They started out, weighted down some, by the extra hundred rounds of ammunition they each carried along with their rifles.

Mack and Kathy weren't carrying anything to make their walk any more difficult. Not even water. Mack knew of a spot near this trail where fresh, clean water bubbled out of the ground. Safe to drink water. It was one of the few natural springs left anywhere near where the refuge was located. It was in a secluded spot that very few people knew about. Because of that, no one had as yet done anything to destroy it. Something Mack knew would happen once it became public knowledge.

They weren't far enough into their walk yet, to need a drink. They were instead stopping frequently to study one life form or another. It didn't matter to Mack what it was, plant or animal, he appreciated it all.

That was especially true now. New species were showing up throughout the refuge since the fire that destroy a huge portion of the life that was once there. The ground was blackened and seemingly dead right after the fire. It was predicted then, by conservatives, Republicans, and Evangelical Christians, that it wouldn't recover within the lifetime of anyone living during the fire.

Now, just a few years later, there was almost no black to be seen. And what was there, was only the few remaining trees that didn't completely burn. The ground, instead of black, was now covered with many shades of green from the multiple species of native grasses growing. Mixed in with them, throughout the refuge, were broadleaf plants of all shapes and sizes.

Brush grew in patches tall enough, and spread out in areas far enough, to hide whole herds of deer. Everywhere the ground was covered with plants that provided food for many of the critters again calling the refuge home. Almost as important, many of them also provided visiting humans the pleasure of seeing the wild flowers they produced. Especially in the spring. when the vivid colors treated the eyes and filled the senses.

As Mack pointed out how the refuge was making a constant recovery, Kathy listened closely to what he said. She often smiled at his explanations. As they moved along she more and more appreciated his enthusiasm for everything he talked about. It wasn't long before she was wondering about going back on tour. Maybe staying here, and getting to know this man and his refuge better would make more sense. And if she did that, she could forever haunt Dale. She was also beginning to believe she might be worthy of forgiveness. If he couldn't deliver it, he might deserve to be haunted. Not only by her, but by the memories of what they once had.

Just as important, she wanted to be close friends with, and spend a lot of time with, Mack and Lisa. And maybe, just maybe, she could eventually find a man half as good as Dale Magee or Mack Thomas. Finding one as good as either one of them, she knew, was impossible.

What she didn't know, was that two men were following them. Two men who believed they were far better men than Dale or Mack. Men who were determined that she would never have the someday she wanted.

CHAPTER 21

Lisa left the table, thanked Ben and Theresa so their usual outstanding breakfast, and opened the door to leave. As she did, an incredible pain hit her deep in her gut. She sat down hard on the floor, and as suddenly as the pain came, pictures of Mack, lying on the ground with his arm stretched out as if to protect something, flashed through her head.

Ben quickly moved to her side to help her. A shocked look filled Wanda's face as she watched Lisa. She turned to Roy. "It's Mack. The visions are back. Lisa's seeing the same thing I am. We need to help him." She struggled up from her chair. "You've got to drive, Roy." She walked over to Lisa, took her arm, and with Ben's help, got her to her feet. "We have to hurry. Mack needs us."

They rushed out of the house, and climbed into Roy's pickup. Lisa was sitting in the middle, because Wanda pushed her into the truck. Her legs were still unable to function normally, and Wanda didn't consider taking the time for Lisa to get in the truck normally. Not when she was sure Mack was in trouble.

And he definitely was in trouble. One of the main things he wanted to show Kathy, was the highest spot in the refuge. It was a small hill, that for some unknown reason, was called Blue Hill. As hills everywhere go, it was an insignificant thing. But for the refuge, it was a special place where a person could see more of the refuge than anywhere else.

Mack and Kathy were on top of Blue Hill, near one side of it. It was a spot that had long ago washed away in a severe thunder storm. The hillside had eroded over the years, so it was no longer the cliff it once was. But it was still too steep to walk up or down on.

Without thinking about what he was doing, Mack put his left arm around her waist, and used his right arm to point out the lakes and ponds they could see from the high ground they were on.

Suddenly a shot rang out. The bullet hit the remnants of an ancient oak tree that somehow survived the fire. It was only inches from Macks head. Mack instinctively pulled Kathy down to the ground to get her out of the line of fire. The problem with his move was the steep hillside. They were too close to it, and when he tackled her, they went over the edge.

He was still clinging to her as they rolled down the rough ground. They made it to the bottom alive, but Kathy's left arm was seriously sprained in the fall. She screamed when Mack grabbed it to pull her up and get her out of there.

He let go of her arm and again put his arm around her, to guide her away from the hill. They managed to hide in some thick brush. After they settled down on their stomachs, they carefully turned around in an attempt to see who it was who was shooting at them.

That proved easier than they expected. The two now frantic men stood in the open ground at the top of the hill, leaving themselves wide open. Mack had little hope of stopping them. His only weapon was a pistol. Not that accurate at that distance. They were carrying AR15s. Weapons of war, designed only for killing people. It was not what could be called a fair fight. Mack knew from experience that he had to try to fight back anyway.

"I've never seen those men," Mack whispered. "Do you know who they are?"

Kathy did her best to identify the men, but because they were constantly moving a fair distance away, it took her a while. When she did, she gasped for breath and nearly fainted.

"I know them, Mack," she said, her voice so low he could barely hear her. "The tall one is my former crew manager. The one I fired. The one I should have stopped when he did what he did to me. The one I was a pure damn fool about. The other guy was part of the road crew. I fired him a couple of years ago. He was lazy and incompetent."

"So now they're upset enough with you to shoot at you?"

"Apparently they're upset with me. But I think they were shooting at you."

"You're probably right. Kill me first. Then do to you whatever they want. I doubt they plan on leaving you alive when they're done with you."

"This is horrible. I'm so sorry, Mack. It wasn't bad enough what I did to Dale. I did this to you too. What are we going to do?"

Mack didn't answer. He took careful aim at the chubby man. He was now the most exposed of the two men. Mack was trying for the center of his chest when he fired twice. Due to the distance, his first bullet hit him in the upper arm. The second was a complete miss. The good thing about it was the fact that the bullet that hit the man sent him reeling down the hill. He landed with a thump and then lay quite still.

Terrance Withers, being the untrustworthy friend and general coward that he was, decided it would be a good idea to run. Mack was shooting at them, and he didn't want to get shot. So he ran. He was ripping up the ground with spinning back wheels, as he left the trailhead parking lot, just as Roy drove in.

The instant he stopped the truck, Wanda was out of it. Lisa was right behind her. She was fully recovered now, and was off down the trail at a hard run. Roy and Wanda were close behind.

By then, Kathy, had taken a close look at Claude Glut and positively identified him. "I don't suppose, Mack," she said, "there's anyway you can avoid calling Dale, is there?"

"No. If this were just a husband, wife thing, we probably could avoid it. But he's still the sheriff. I just shot a man. So there's no way around it. We have to call 911, and that's sure to involve Dale."

"Damn it all. I don't think I should have come back home. I didn't think Dale would forgive me, or give me a second chance. So I should have known better. All I am anymore is a long list of stupid mistakes."

"Not really, Kathy. You would have been an easier target on the road than what you are here. So it isn't all bad."

"You're probably right. But facing Dale under these circumstances is the last thing I want to do now."

A terrified Lisa reached the top of the hill then. Her voice wasn't much more than a choking gasp, but she still managed to call out their names. Mack yelled his answer. "Down here."

Lisa poked her head over the edge of the eroded ground. "Are you okay?"

"Yes and no," Mack told her. "Kathy's got a badly sprained arm, and there's a man with a bullet in him. He's bleeding, so I guess I better take a look at him. I'd appreciate if you'd call 911. Maybe Dale too, seeing as how his wife's involved in all this."

Mack was well aware of the tone of sarcasm in his voice when he made his comment about Kathy being Dale's wife. He didn't really want to do that to Lisa or anyone else, but he was deeply frustrated now. He knew that Dale wouldn't take what happened lightly. But he wasn't at all in the mood to put up with anyone laying judgements down. Not for any reason.

He also was afraid that all of what had happened recently, could damage the friendship he and Dale had. Before he could think about that much, they heard the first sirens. Mack couldn't help but wonder. Would Dale be as concerned about Kathy as he should be? Or would he try to pretend that what happened to her wasn't anything personal.

As soon as Roy and Wanda knew that things were more or less under control, Roy walked back to the trail head to meet the sheriff's cars as they arrived. He also asked the first deputy to arrive to call for a couple of ambulances.

Mack had Claude awake and sitting up when the first deputy got to Kathy, Lisa, and Mack. He had the bleeding in his arm stopped, and Lisa had made a temporary sling from Mack's shirt for Kathy's sprained arm.

Dale looked decidedly unhappy when he got there. When Mack saw the look on his face, he held up his hand and shook his head no. "This is my fault, Dale," he said. "So lay off the speeches to Kathy. I wasn't paying attention. I was too damn busy showing off this refuge. If you need to bitch, do it to me. She already feels bad enough. There's no point in making it worse."

Dale didn't argue with Mack. He asked what happened, then listened as Mack explained it. When Mack finished, Dale asked Kathy, "What are you going to do now? With that Terrance bastard still out there, I don't think you should go back on the road yet. It's too dangerous."

"Can I stay at the house? You're the sheriff. If you can't keep me safe, no one can."

Dale looked a little lost she made that request. "I'm not sure that's a good idea, given our current circumstances. "

"What?" Kathy said. "Do you think now, that I'm so evil I'll contaminate the house by being there?" The anger in her voice was harsh and loud. "Do you hate me that goddamn bad now Dale? So be it. You feel that way, I'll take my chances on the road. It's obvious that what happens in the rest of my life, is none of your concern."

"I'm sorry, Kathy. I didn't mean it that way. It's just that as long as we are going to get divorced the way you wanted us too. it's better if we don't do anything that could lead to any kind of further involvement."

"You can stay with us," Lisa told her. She glared at Dale as she talked. She made no attempt to hide the fact that she hated what he was doing. She, along with everyone who was in any way involved with Dale and Kathy, now considered him more wrong than she was. "There is no way we are going to let you get hurt. Not for any reason."

"That's right, Kathy," Mack added to Lisa's invitation. "You are more than welcome to stay with us. For however long it takes to catch the son of a bitch who's hurt you as much as he has."

Dale was feeling small now. The truth was, he wanted Kathy to stay with him. He wanted to forgive her and welcome her home. But his ridiculous male pride wouldn't let him. And that meant he was close to making, what could turn out to be, the biggest mistake of his life.

CHAPTER 22

Mack and Paul were in the office, going over the case of slaughtered dogs and cats. Lisa, Wanda, and Roy were out, checking all of the places they thought it might be possible to find Terrance Withers hiding. Kathy was visiting with Ben and Theresa while everyone else was busy. Spending time with them was something Kathy was enjoying. Theresa was her aunt, her mother's sister, and by visiting this way she was hoping to learn more about Ben, as well as Theresa. It meant that for the time the three were out and about, she was satisfied with the way she was spending her time.

Lisa was out there looking because of what she considered Terrance to be. Which was a control freak rapist. She was also very fond of Kathy, and believed she deserved whatever help Lisa could give her.

Wanda was there for the same reasons, along with the fact that he'd tried to kill Mack. That was something Wanda simply couldn't abide by. Next to Roy, she considered Mack to be the best man she'd ever known. He was her best friend too. So even though she was very much concerned about Kathy, she wanted some retaliation for what he attempted to do to Mack and Kathy.

Roy was there for all the same reasons as Lisa and Wanda. But even more, he was there to try to keep the two of them out of trouble. He knew that this hunt was more personal to them than all but a few other cases they might work on could or would be. That left a greater chance for them to make an error. It didn't matter who a person was, when emotions were involved, errors in judgement were often more likely.

With the three of them out hunting, it left the animal case up to Mack and Paul. It was a situation, that earlier in their investigation of it, would have slowed it considerably. At this stage of it though, the effect of their not being involved was considerably less.

Another thing that eased the lack of help from the three was the fact that they still had Sue. She was always busy with technical problems connected to various cases they were handling, but she never failed to assist anyone in the agency when they really needed her and her expertise.

Right at the moment though, Paul and Mack didn't need her. Enough evidence had already been gathered to keep them busy, going over and organizing it. for the rest of the day.

Along with that work in front of them, they had a meeting with Dan Tucker, the man who got them involved in the case in the first place. Mack knew what the meeting would be about. It would cover two things. Number one being the contract they had with Dan.

He hadn't made the last payment when it was due. A problem Mack had anticipated when they started the case. He was sure at the time they agreed to take it on that it would be far more complicated than it appeared to be at that time. So he expected it would cost more than Dan would be able to afford. The money didn't concern Mack though.

Refuge Rescuers Detective agency had a trust fund, set up by a billionaire supporter, to cover worthy cases that the people who wanted to hire them couldn't afford. The reason the agency took his money to start with, is because before they decided to handle a case at all, they needed to be sure the problem was legitimate. In this case it most definitely was.

The second reason for the meeting was the same as most of their meetings with clients. What have they learned so far. Mack was ready to deal with both problems when Dan arrived.

Julie was at the receptionist desk when he came in. She was expecting him, so she surprised him with a wide, friendly smile when she greeted him. He was expecting a frown at best, since he hadn't make the last payment. And wouldn't have been shocked to have her demand a payment before she allowed him to see Mack and Paul.

Instead, she said, "It's good to see you again, Mister Tucker. Mack and Paul will be with you shortly. If you will follow me, I'll show you the way to the meeting room." Once he was sitting down in the room, she asked him, "can I get you anything? Coffee? A can of soda pop? Or water?"

That was another thing he definitely didn't expect, so it took him a moment to answer. "A Coke or Pepsi would sure taste good right now."

She returned with a can of Pepsi and a glass, then left him. He poured the pop into his glass, and as he was about to take his first sip, Mack and Paul joined him. He quickly set his glass down, and stood to greet them. Mack set an envelope down on the table where he was sitting, then stretched out his arm so they could shake hands. Paul followed with his own hand shake.

"Before we get into the case itself," Mack said, "we need to discuss the financial part of it."

"Here it comes," thought Dan. "The complaints about the missed payment."

"To start with," Mack explained, "it has turned out to be far bigger, and far worse, than any of us could have possibly expected. The costs, have of course, also run much higher. Way beyond what anyone could normally be expected to cover."

"I suppose that means then," Dan said, relieved that Mack hadn't as yet asked for money. But at the same time, disappointed that it sounded like they were going to drop the case. He continued his answer, "that you're going to be forced to quit you investigation of the dead animals?"

"No." Mack smiled. He did it both because he was going to enjoy telling Dan what he was about to say. He also did it to help relax Dan some. His nervousness was growing ever more apparent. "We will not be stopping the investigation for financial reasons. We will be doing everything we possibly can to bring the matter to a decent, and hopefully fair, conclusion."

He paused for a moment, and turned to Paul. "You can give it to him, Paul."

Paul smiled, and took a check out of a pocket of his suit coat and handed it to Dan. "It's a complete reimbursement of all the fees you have paid us so far. We do, however, expect your full involvement in the case in the future. To bring it to the conclusion we will be working for, we might need your help with any number of things. One of them could be something you might find distasteful. A court appearance, where you will be questioned by some nasty attorneys for the other side. Are you willing to do that?"

"Hell yes. There ain't much I won't do to get the bastards who killed all those dogs and cats. Sometimes I wake up at night, sweating because I was dreaming about them poor critters. Whoever did it to them, is damn well some kind of sick."

"That's good to hear. All of us here, find that what's been going on abhorrent. We are determined to put a stop to it. And also lay some kind of penalty on the guilty party or parties."

"I have to say," Dan said, "you guys are a surprise. Giving me my money back and still working on solving the case goes way past anything I'd ever expected. And before I forget what's important, thank you so much for the check. I hate to admit it, but I really do need the money."

"I can understand that," Mack answered. "Given the way the rich almost always seem to manage to keep wages down. Even in an independent business like the one you work in. So, are you ready now, to hear about your case?"

"I sure am. But why did you call it my case? You just gave me my money back."

"Because as far as we're all concerned it still is your case. You're the one who brought it to our attention. We expect you to stay involved. So yes, it still is your case."

"Well thank you. You make me proud to be part of it. So, where are you with it?"

"So far, the good news is, we have a lot of proof to show who's responsible. The biggest problem is the law. There's no way in criminal court that we can get them punished adequately for what they've done. Even if they're found guilty of the crimes they've committed, it's likely they'll only get a slap on the wrist. More than likely a fine for a relatively small sum of money."

"How small?"

"The amount might seem like a lot of money to you or me. But however much it is, it won't have much if any affect on them. In civil court though, if we do it right and we win, the numbers could reach into the billions."

"Who would get that kind of money if you do win?"

"A lot of people, Dan. What we're going to try to do is put together the right team of lawyers, and start a class action suit. We'll try to involve every person possible, who's had a pet disappear in the past couple of years. There's a lot of figuring and a lot of technical work still to be done, but the numbers, when all is said and done, could easily reach the billions. If I have my way, it will turn out to be enough to bankrupt one of the largest drug companies in the world."

"That sounds good, except for one thing. Won't it cause a hardship for a lot of people if they go bankrupt? Won't people need the pills they make?"

"The pills won't stop. The bankruptcy will raise hell with their financials for a while, but they'll stay in business. What

I'm hoping for is that the current management gets fired, and we have enough evidence to have them tried in criminal court as individuals. Not part of a corporate structure. I want the bastards in jail. If they end up fired, I'm hoping they will be liable for the deaths of the animals. Liable enough to be sued individually. But that will be up to the lawyers and the law."

"All I can say now," Dan said with twinkling eyes and a big smile, "is that if any of what you're trying to do happens, I'll be satisfied."

Paul spoke up now. "There's one more thing, Dan. When lawyers take on a case like this and win, they often pay a finders fee. That will be part of the contract we have when we put the group together. It will, in this case if they win, amount to millions of dollars. Since you brought the case to our attention, you are as far as we are concerned, going to receive part of the finders fee."

'You are kidding me?"

"No. Don't hold your breath, but your share could easily reach over a million.'

"Why are you telling me about this? You could have kept all the money. I never would have know the difference."

"That's simple. It would be the wrong thing to do. One thing we'd like to see from you though, if all this works out. Take some of the money, however much it is, and help someone who really needs help. We don't need to know anything about it, one way or the other. But it would be a good thing to do."

"I'll try to do right with it. After what you guys are trying to do, how could I do anything else."

Dan left the office then. Paul and Mack went back to work, struggling with all the problems facing them. Accomplishing what they wanted to with this case was not going to be an easy task, and they very well knew it.

CHAPTER 23

As the day neared its end, Mack and Paul decided that they, and everyone connected to Refuge Rescuers deserved a relaxing evening. One that included a good meal that no one needed to cook or clean up after. So they set the meeting time via cell phone, and Mack and Paul put together the riding arrangements to the bar.

Kathy rode with Ben and Theresa, following behind Paul and Julie. Mack, Lisa, and Sue brought up the rear of the three vehicle convoy. They weren't actually expecting any problems on the way. With Kathy in the middle vehicle, it would be very difficult for Terrance Withers to do anything. It would take a lot of help, and a lot of guns for him to get to her.

Mack was on edge anyway. Something that he couldn't put his finger on, started eating at him as soon as they drove on the county road that took them to the Mystic Curve Inn. The bar where they planned to eat. So he was more aware of his surroundings than he normally might have been.

As were all of the people who were going to eat supper with him this evening, he was concerned about Terrance and what he might do next. At the same time, his gut was telling him that he was missing something. It was almost like the thought, the knowledge of something he should be paying attention to, was standing in an open door to his brain, but refusing to come out.

They were close to halfway to their destination when Sue's cell phone rang. She answered with a hello, paused a moment, then said, "I'll tell him."

"Who was that?" Mack asked her right away.

"Wanda." Sue looked at him, her expression making it clear she was more than a little curious about something. "She said for you to be real damn careful. She didn't know for sure why, but she knew without a doubt, you had better be careful."

"Damn," Mack answered. "They're coming back."

"What are you talking about, Mack? Is there something between you and Wanda we all should know about? I know it might not be any of my business, but what the hell is going on with you two?"

Agitated or not, Mack couldn't hold back his smile. "I don't know what it is exactly, Sue. But Wanda and I have some kind of psychic connection. It seems to come and go. Sometimes it's about one of us. Other times, someone we know. Occasionally it's about someone connected to something we are both involved in. We both get premonitions. Most often it's nighttime dreams. Lately though, they can come anytime."

"Well, she said for you to be extra careful. Why don't you have the same feelings now?"

Mack gave Sue another smile. This time a grim one. "Thing is," he explained, "I do. So don't let anything surprise you. It's possible for something to go wrong before we get there. If something does, you be ready to hit the floor."

"Just like that? I should be ready to *hit* the floor. I want you to know, Mack, I am damn tired of getting into places and circumstances where I feel so defenseless. So I'm warning you right now, starting tomorrow, you are going begin my training. I want to become a private detective. If for no other reason than I will gain the ability to defend myself, the same as Lias and Wanda."

"What about the tech work?"

"Of course I'll continue with that. But I also want to be able to handle myself well enough, so I don't ever need to do this hit the floor again. Instead, I want to be able to assist you with the trouble, whatever it might be."

"I can't say I'm either happy or upset about that idea, Sue. I'll have to think about it before I can comment on my own feelings. But I do have a tremendous amount of respect for you, so I will do everything I can to help you become a detective. But in the meantime, it'll be a good idea if you keep an eye out for the sign of any kind of trouble."

"I will, but I'm not at all sure what to look for."

"I'm not totally sure either. Just look out for anything out of the ordinary. Something as simple as a car parked where one normally wouldn't be. Anything you see. I doesn't matter how small. Cockroaches can sometimes squeeze into some pretty small places."

"Cockroaches, Mack. I know they are pretty much totally hated by all humans. But compared to the man who is after Kathy right now, they can be kind of warm and cuddly little creatures. Cockroaches in the wrong place can screwup any space where we live. But it's nothing compared to what they are trying to do to Kathy now. Or what they did to Lisa when she was still just a kid."

"You'll get no argument from me on that, Sue. None at all."

They didn't speak again for the rest of a very tense ride. Sue felt a sense of relief when they finally got to the Mystic Curve Inn, and were settled at a table with everyone else. Mack wasn't. Nor was Wanda. Lisa too, had a sense of foreboding.

After all the initial greetings, Mack made a decision about what was happening. He wanted to, if possible, hold any problems or violence off. So he called Dale on his private cell phone. Dale listened patiently to what Mack told him. When Mack asked for an escort for Kathy on the ride home, Dale agreed.

When Mack suggested that Dale join them for the meal, to add to Kathy's protection in the bar, he objected. "That wouldn't be a good idea,"

he said.

"I think we should be past that now," Mack argued. "No matter how you or I or any of us feels, it's her safety that matters. And I for one, would feel a lot better about her safety. with you sitting at our table with your uniform on."

"Do you have any idea, Mack?" Dale argued back, "Just how uncomfortable I would feel if I was there."

"You'll get over that a whole lot quicker than you will get over it if she gets hurt or worse."

"Damn you, Mack, I hate it when you get so logical. Okay, I'll come. But please, leave it go at that."

"I'll try."

Lisa said it first, when Mack hung up. "That Dale?"

"It was. He's going to join us."

Kathy gave Mack the biggest frown she could manage. "I don't think you needed to invite him. I don't think anything is going to happen, so we won't need him."

Wanda spoke up now. "I'm sorry, Kathy, but you are mistaken. Something is going to happen. It might or might not be about you. And if it is, it might be directly or indirectly about you. That's not what's most important right now though. What is, is the fact that something is going to go down and it is going to affect Mack for sure, and you maybe."

"How could you know that for sure?" Kathy asked.

"She knows, and so do I," Mack said. "So let's all be decent, and show Dale the respect and friendship he deserves when he gets here."

The rest of the time at the bar played out okay, but didn't offer anyone the relaxing evening Mack hoped for when he organized it. Dale sat as far from Kathy as he could at their table, so they didn't talk at all during the meal.

The most tension they felt during the time there, was when a group of five strangers, all men, sat down at a table close by. They made the same motions and finger pointing to show that they noticed all of the females at their own table, but it stopped there.

When it was time to go, Dale quietly went out with everyone else. Since Paul was going home, which was a few miles away from where everyone but Julie was going, he took her home too. Roy led the convoy home. Wanda and Sue followed, with the car carrying Ben, Theresa, and Kathy behind them. Dale was next, then Lisa, and Mack at the very end.

As they drove through the now dark, moonless night, Mack's apprehension over the safety of everyone but himself constantly grew. He couldn't shake the feeling that he, not Kathy, was the target this time. He wasn't at all sure why. Only that someone very much wanted to get him. So he lagged back as much as he could without alarming Lisa.

If he was the target, he didn't want her in the line of fire. Or anyone else if he could help it. As he drove, he let part of his brain drift through the events of the evening, bring to find something he might have missed. Two things, both that seemed insignificant at the time, hit him together.

First thing he was aware of now, was the five guys at the nearby table. When Mack and the rest of them stood to leave, one of the men picked up his cell phone and made a call. The second thing he'd watched while they all loaded up in their vehicles, were two men standing outside the bar. They were smoking, and one was talking on his cellphone. He turned to watch them get in their vehicles.

All the men wore the same red baseball hats, with the word Pride on them. Mack slapped his forehead. How the hell could he have missed that? The Pride Guys. He shot one of them when he and Kathy were attacked while walking in the refuge. Claude Glut was the wounded man.

He had bragged, long and loud about being a member of The Pride Guys. And he'd announced to everyone who was forced to deal with him, how he'd never be in jail long. Most of all, he'd made no secret that Mack was on their list of people who were going to have to die. He was, in fact, at the top of their list. They hadn't, as yet, announced who else was on it.

Mack couldn't concern himself about that though. There was nothing left to do, but prepare for their attack. He hoped that the convoy would be enough to scare them off, but his experience with people as limited in intelligence as The Pride Guys obviously were, were probably too stupid to figure out what the attack might cost them.

The first of the Guys pulled out of a farm road in front of Mack. They were in a half ton pickup. Two men rode in the cab, two in the bed. It was a foreign model, and slightly underpowered. It wasn't equipped with a rear bumper, which made it particularly vulnerable to Mack's truck.

He drove a Ford F250. A full one ton truck. Its front bumper was heavily braced with specially designed steel bars, that held together even after a heavy impact. A steel grid in front of the grille guarded the radiator. The glass in the truck was bullet proof all the way around. The rear bumper had the same bracing as the front.

The two men in the truck bed held AR15s, redesigned to fire full automatic. When they fired, it made a hell of a racket, but the bullets did little harm to Mack's windshield. In response, he slammed his accelerator to the floor. His truck, superior in every way, slammed hard into the rear of the Pride Guy pickup. As Mack's front bumper locked onto the backend of it, he gave his steering wheel just enough of a twitch to start the pickup in front of him into a spin. As it swerved to the side of the road, now facing the opposite direction, it came to the edge of the ditch. The front wheels jammed to the right, and the truck flipped into the ditch, then rolled over. The two men in the truck bed flew into the air, then landed in the ditch just ahead of their truck. It landed directly on top of them, crushing the life out of them.

The men in the cab of the truck didn't get low enough, fast enough. One suffered a broken back. The other a broken neck. Unfortunately for them, by the time everything settle down enough, the ambulance arrived too late. They both died on the way to the hospital.

They might have survived if they medics could have gotten to them faster, but a second pickup slowed everything down. It came out of a farm road behind Mack. The Pride Guy driving was sure he had Mack now. After all, what could a lowlife liberal do against a macho man who was part of The Pride Guys.

Unfortunately for them, it was a lot. And the man with the intellect of a four year old was about to find that out. Mack didn't bother to play any games with the truck behind him. He used the superior power of the engine in his truck and pulled far enough ahead to make a sliding, spinning U-turn.

He pulled his semiautomatic from its shoulder holster. He held it in his left hand after he powered down the window on his side. The other pickup pulled hard to its right to avoid him as he went by it. Both trucks were traveling at a high rate of speed as they passed each other. Mack managed to fire several times as he went by anyway. One bullet found its target. It hit the driver of the pickup in the chest. It didn't kill him, but it did disable him. He, and the men riding with him landed hard in the ditch.

They were shaken hard enough to allow Mack to get to them before they could do anything to retaliate. He had them face down on the ground and their weapons confiscated by the time Dale got back to him. Sirens could be heard by then too.

Dale then gave Mack, what was for him, a rare smile. "You damn sure, Mack," he said, "haven't lost your touch, have you?"

"Depends on how you look at it. I should have picked up on those people back at the bar, not at this late date."

"Wouldn't have mattered much, Mack. You didn't have any reason to go after them then. They had just as much right to be there as you did."

"I don't know. It seems like I should have been able to do something."

"Again, you did all you could. And you've been keeping Kathy safe. For that, I'll be eternally grateful."

"You know as well as I do, Dale, that it should be you doing it. Not me. You two still love each other. You'd be a pure damn fool to throw that away. I know she made a mistake. A really big mistake. But we all make them. And she's a good person at heart. She deserves another chance."

"I know, Mack. And I'm trying. But what she did cut awful deep."

"The only reason she let it happen, was because she felt at the time that it was punishment for what she'd already done to you. It wasn't for the normal reason. So, damnit, Dale, do the right thing while you still have the chance. You wait too long and you'll lose her. You do, and you probably won't get another chance with her. And I can guaranty that you will regret it for the rest of your life."

"I know that, Mack. but give me a few more days. I really do want to work it out with her. You can tell her that too."

"Lisa and I, along with everyone else, will do our best to keep her safe. But when she decides it's time to get back on tour, I can't stop her."

"I thought she said she was going to end the tour?"

"No. She said she would end it for you. If she thinks you two are for sure done, she's going to leave. I doubt she'll ever come back. And it won't take long after that, and your chances with her will be over."

"I understand, Mack," a now solemn Dale said. He went back to work, organizing all the support people working at the crime scene. By the time he finished, Mack was the only one of his group still there. He had to stay to answer the endless questions about what happened, because he was the only one directly involved in it. It took a while to explain to the state police why he was attacked, and how he managed to defeat so many men in two different trucks. In the end, it was Dale's help with the explanations that made the difference.

It was late when Mack finally got home. Lisa was already in bed, but Kathy was sitting on the couch, waiting for him. "I know you talked too Dale," she said. "Did he say anything about me?"

"He did. I'm tired enough now though, that I don't remember all of it."

"Will you tell me what you do remember?"

"Only that he wants to reconcile your differences, and for you guys to get back together. But it's going to take a while."

"I hate to say this, Mack, but I no longer believe it should. I was wrong. I screwed up royally. But what happened, what I did, is over now. So you tell him that if he doesn't want it to end, then he better say so. Directly to me. I'm not going to wait much longer. If I don't have him, I'm going to settle for my career. I've damaged it enough already, to wait much longer."

"I understand, Kathy. I'll tell him. And I'll tell him, just like I'm going to tell you now, it'll be one hell of a waste if you two don't work it out."

"You're right about that, Mack." She shocked him then, and moved close to him. Her arms curled around his neck and their lips met. The kiss was long and memorable. "That's more than just a thank you for everything, Mack. It was my way way of telling you how it is. Dale just better get his shit together."

He watched her as she turned away. Then he watched her walk down the hall to the bedroom. He went into his own bedroom them. He stripped down and went into the shower. He ran the water as hot as he could stand. He rubbed hard as he dried himself.

He didn't dress before he got into bed next to Lisa. She was wearing the same clothes he was. he pulled her close and held her tight as he fell asleep. She was awake just enough to be real glad he was home safe.

Kathy fell asleep and into a dream about holding someone's hand, while walking in a wild place. It was okay though. Holding hands was enough. At least for now.

CHAPTER 24

It was first meeting with the team of lawyers put together for the class action lawsuit against Davis Drug. They met in a meeting room of the firm where the two lead lawyers were partners. Mack, Paul, and Wanda met with them. Lisa stayed at the office, so she would be close by if Kathy needed her for anything. Roy and Sue were doing research on The Pride Guys. They were a national organization, so they all knew there was a good chance of more trouble from them.

Trouble or not though, the three were forced to concentrate on the meeting they were in. It was going to take a lot of persuasion, they knew, to convince the lawyers to take on the lawsuit. The amount of work needed to put it together was almost overwhelming. And that was just the beginning. They would need a near perfect presentation to convince a jury to award the amount of money they would be asking for.

On the positive side, a tremendous percentage of people, from all walks of life, had pets. And most of them loved their pets as if they were part of the family. So they were not going to sympathize with anyone, corporation or not, that so indiscriminately slaughtered so many of them.

It helped too, that a lot of the dead animals did start out as someones pet. Pets stolen from backyard kennels, or dogs and cats who were allowed to run free, regardless of how short a time. Refuge Rescuers had already been in contact with many of them.

Another group unhappy about the dog slaughter were the breeders. Even the ones who were paid for their animals were decidedly unhappy about the way they were ultimately treated. There were hundreds more situations still to be checked out.

Along with all that, every animal protection organization that knew of the pending lawsuit wanted, one way or the other, to be involved.

Mack did a good job of presenting all of the evidence Refuge Rescuers managed to gather during to course of their investigation. It was so good, in fact, that the lawyers were very much impressed. Especially one of the two leaders of the group.

"I have to tell you, Mack, that I don't just appreciate the way you've made your case. You've solved a mystery that's been bothering my daughter for over a year now. Her dog went missing one night. For eight years she let him out to do his thing just before bed. We have a large, fenced yard, so it was never a problem. For no apparent reason, he disappeared one night. It broke her heart. Everyone in the family was broken up about it, actually. Now, we at least know why."

The second lead spoke up then. "We'll let you know in the next day or two what our decision is. But I can tell you now, at least two of us are already in favor of going ahead with it."

They got firm handshakes from all the lawyers before they left them. It was a small thing, but it came across as something positive. They were fairly confident that they now had their team of lawyers.

Their confidence proved to be accurate. It didn't take a day or two for the lawyers to decide. Mack was notified of their decision to take on the class action lawsuit by late that afternoon.

By the end of the next day, the lawyers had a system setup to make contact with pet owners and everyone who had lost an animal or animals. They also organized a group to interview everyone who they contacted, that they possibly could.

A few days after the initial meeting with the lawyers, the media picked up on the story. Davis Drug was named in nearly all the stories on television and in newspapers. The story spread like a virus throughout the internet, and stayed around, rather than disappearing the way so many stories did.

The publicity proved to be a big asset for the lawyers, when it came to finding additional people who lost pets. It nearly buried Refuge Rescuers in phone calls from people wanting to hire them for things that ran from trivial to impossible. Most of them things they had no interest in handling.

The call that bothered Mack the most was the one from Davis Drug. They wanted Mack, Lisa, and Paul to come their headquarters for a meeting. At first, Paul and Lisa were willing to meet with them there. Mack absolutely refused.

"It they want to meet," he said, "it is damn well going to be in a neutral place. One that we pick. They don't want to go along with that, there will not be any meeting."

After a couple of days of negotiations, they agreed on a restaurant located on the four lane, about ten miles south of Kingsburg. Davis Drug made the arrangements, and the meeting was scheduled to take place over a dinner meal. It was also to be held in one of their banquet rooms. They wanted it private.

Because he didn't at all trust the drug company, Sue came along for the meeting. When they got there, she immediately scanned the room for any kind of recording devices. She found six of them right away. They had agreed there wouldn't be any there.

Mack didn't tell them to remove the devices. Instead, Sue quickly installed a dozen devices of various kinds. Half of them video cameras, setup to capture the meeting from various angles. The rest of the devices she setup were audio. Sensitive enough to record every sound in the room. No matter how small.

Davis Drug didn't know it, but Mack had hoped from the beginning that they would do exactly what they did. It gave Refuge Rescuer's the excuse they wanted, for setting up their own surveillance of the meeting. Mack, Paul, Wanda, and Sue were there to represent their detective agency.

They remained quiet after Sue finished her work, and it was time to start the meeting. It took a few minutes for the lead attorney for Davis Drug to speak.

"We invited you to this meeting to discuss your involvement with the class action suit involving the deaths of a few animals." He paused and looked at Mack. "We have learned that you people, and the firm you work for, have had a lot to do with putting it together. Actually, it's our belief that you were the ones who got it started."

Mack responded to his comment. A comment that was meant to be an accusation. The man who made it also considered himself to be representing a company with a lot of power and influence. And his law firm was also powerful and influential. All that meant that he too was powerful. Powerful enough to be in complete charge of the meeting they were having. So his tone of voice when he made the comment was one of a threat.

Mack's answer to it was, "Yes, that is true. What's also true is the fact that we don't intend to stop doing it. Not until Davis Drug pays dearly for what they've done. And if it's ever possible, the management of the company have all been locked up in jail where they belong."

"Now that would be a pointless miscarriage of justice, if there ever was one. Those people are, and always have been, dedicated to the service of humanity. That is why they have worked so diligently to consistently develop new drugs, which have improved the lives of so many."

"Right. And they've all gotten filthy rich doing it."

"Any money they've made, they've earned. Few people have worked as hard as the leaders of the drug industry. And that's what they've been doing with the animals. Everyone involved is concerned about the new viruses attacking many different animals. But especially dogs and cats. Davis Drug has simply been seriously seeking a cure."

"Sure. And they've killed what now appears to be several thousand dogs and cats while doing it. There are better ways of finding cure than the way they're doing it."

"Maybe, but ways too slow to deal with the emergency we are now facing."

"The emergency you need to stop," Mack said, his impatience growing with every word spoken. "is the slaughter of animals that don't deserve to die such a painful death. So it's time for you to get to the point of this meeting. I know there's more to it than trying to convince me that Davis Drug is right in what it's doing."

"That's one thing we can agree on." He gave Mack a half smile. One that he was sure showed his superior intellect as much as the fact that he was agreeing with Mack on something. "We are here to convince you that finding the cure is the most important side to any and all of the issues. We want to make you, and your agency, an offer to demonstrate how serious we are about finding that cure."

"I'll bet you are," Mack answered, unable to hold back the heavy sarcasm in his voice.

The Lawyer didn't like his response. "You could, you know, listen to our offer before you answer with that tone of voice."

"I think it would be a good idea for you to say what you've got to say, while we're still here to listen. Because if you come at me with your homosuperior tone of voice again, we will be out of here."

"If it wasn't for the strong desire of the management if Davis Drug to put this issue behind them, that is exactly what I would suggest."

Mack was close to walking out. He stayed, only because he was more curious about what their offer might be, than he was angry with the puppet talking to him. He also wanted to record it when the offer was made. So he sat silent, waiting for the offer.

"Again," the man said, "this offer is only being made to illustrate how sincere they are in wanting to resolve this issue."

Again, Mack was silent as he waited to hear about the offer.

The lawyer momentarily stared at Mack, now exasperated with his silence. Finally he sighed and said, "Davis Drug is prepared to offer you, and your detective agency, one full million dollars to remove yourselves from participating in any way in the lawsuit."

As it nearly always seemed to be, the issue was entirely about money. And since this issue was about what it might cost Davis Drug, which was a lot of money, they were hoping a million dollar bribe would keep Refuge Rescuers out of it. Something that they were sure would greatly increase their chances of winning a court battle.

Mack's immediate reaction was to walk out of the meeting. Their bribe offer was, more than anything else, an insult. It meant that the people from Davis Drug, who were behind the slaughter of so many animals, thought Mack and all the rest of Refuge Rescuers wanted nothing more than to make a quick buck.

"The thing is," Mack answered the man, "we aren't in this for the money. What we want is for Davis Drug and the creeps who run it, to pay for what they've done. Just killing all those completely innocent animals would have been enough to get us involved. But every step of the way they've lied, cheated, stolen from people, and hurt a lot of people. And the hell of it is, for right now, they're still doing it."

"You should be more careful what you accuse people of doing. Don't forget, we've recorded this meeting. It'll be easy enough to show the world how dishonest you've been all along.

We have the experts who will take the recordings we have and make you look like nothing but bad."

Mack laughed at him now. "We've recorded it all too. Including what you just said. So all we have to do is show a video of this entire meeting to prove what all of you are really about. So stick your million dollars up your ass. And tell the management of Davis Drugs that we have every intention of seeing their asses hung out to dry."

Sue, with the assistance of everyone in their group, quickly gathered together all of her equipment, along with the recordings of the meeting. They left the meeting. When they reached the lot where their cars were parked, Sue sat in her car and downloaded three different recordings on to her laptop, then transmitted them to other, protected sites. First, they went to her office, then to the lawyers working on the lawsuit, and finally to a site that would be difficult to trace.

The rest of the recordings were downloaded to her laptop, and from there to a couple of USB flash drives. Mack and Paul each took possession of one of those.

Confident now, that there was no way the people representing Davis Drug could steal or destroy the recordings of the meeting, they left for home.

CHAPTER 25

After losing eight members of their group to one man when they attacked him The Pride Guys, even as dense as they were, realized that they were up against a formidable enemy. But that only made their lust to kill Mack stronger. So they carefully watched him.

After several days, they decided that the best way to get to him would be through someone vulnerable that he cared about. Because they considered all women to be nothing but creatures to provide them sexual satisfaction, they were sure that any of females he cared about were vulnerable to their predation.

Capturing one of them should be, as far as they were concerned, an easy task. It didn't matter either, if they found two or three of them together. They still shouldn't be any kind of a problem. No woman, or group of women, could stand up to The Pride Guys.

So when the day came that Kathy decided she very much wanted to do something with her hair, Lisa and Wanda went with her to the local beauty shop, where she could have it cut and permed. They were still concerned about Terrance Withers, so they kept a sharp eye out for him, or anyone who came across as suspicious.

The Pride Guys managed to track their movements all the way to the beauty shop without realizing that their tracker was spotted. The shop was an independent operation, located in the walkout basement of a beautician's home. It was located in the outskirts of Kingsburg. She only had one assistant, and it was frequently difficult to get an appointment with her, because she was so well known for the quality of her work.

Kathy managed to get one because of who she was. Especially after she more or less explained her situation without going into too many details.

The Pride Guys knew that the number of people they could use for the abduction would have to be limited. If there were too many of them, it would attract too much attention. And that could lead to police involvement. Something they didn't want.

So five of them got into a SUV and drove to the beauty shop that one of their members had followed Kathy, Wanda, and Lisa to. As soon as they arrived there, the one who did the following of them left. She was good at things like following people, or setting traps for them. But when it came to the violence the men loved so much, she tried to avoid it. The sight of blood made her sick. But most of all, The Pride Guys weren't paying her enough to get anymore involved that she already was. They regularly paid her more for sex than she was getting for this job.

What The Pride Guys didn't know, and weren't bright enough to check, or even think about checking, was Lisa's background. Wanda did the driving to the beauty shop, with Kathy in the front seat beside her. Lisa rode in the back, and kept a close eye on everything that went on around them. She knew they were being followed shortly after they left home. Her time as deputy sheriff had taught her a lot about how to pick up on something like being followed.

She told Wanda what was going on, and finished with, "Keep on going all the way to the beauty shop. When we get there, we are going inside like nothing's wrong. When I figure out where the guys are hiding, and waiting for us to come out, I'm going to find out what they want from us. Why they are after us."

"How are you going to do that alone?" Kathy asked, surprised that Lisa would consider such a thing.

"There are a lot of ways to do it. I won't know which one I'll use until the time comes to do it."

"I still don't see how you can do it. You will be all alone. It's too dangerous. We should go home and call the sheriff's office. Let them take care of it. That's what they're for. To protect us."

"You don't need to worry, Kathy. Wanda will be in the shop the whole time."

"But it still doesn't make any sense to me that you should have to do that alone. Why are you doing it?"

"I want to know who is coming after us and why they are coming after us. Is it your boyfriend Terrance, The Pride Guys, or someone we don't know about yet? Over all, we'll be safer if we know, then we will be if we don't. If the police get involved first, we will have less chance of finding that out."

"I still wish you wouldn't try to do this. And damnit, Terrance isn't my boyfriend. He is now my worst enemy."

"As he should be. But he's someone you should remember, if you ever decide to get another boyfriend."

"You can be mean sometimes, Lisa." Kathy was hurt by her words, and close to tears.

"I know. And I don't always like myself when I say things like that. But that doesn't change what is. And what is, is the likely fact that we are here, directly or indirectly as a result of your mistake. And as much as I can understand how it all happened and do not hold it against you, it will be a good thing for you to never forget the how and why of the whole thing."

"That, Lisa, is something that no matter how badly I want to, I will never forget. But I still don't want you to go after those men alone."

"I know. And it's my guess, that even if she isn't saying anything, Wanda doesn't either. But she knows it needs to be done. And she knows I can take care of myself."

"I'm not going to talk you out of it, am I Lisa?"

"No, Kathy, you sure aren't."

They reached the beauty shop then. They parked the car in the driveway near the house, and took the wide walkway around the back. Kathy and Wanda went inside. Lisa used the heavily landscaped backyard to move away from the house. She found a spot near the rear portion of the yard that at the same time gave her some cover, and a view of most of the road in front of the house.

It didn't take long for The Pride Guys to get there. They were so confident in themselves and their abilities to handle three defenseless women, that they just parked on the street in front of the house. When they did, it didn't occur to them that a beauty shop wasn't something that women were always likely to quickly pop in and out of. It didn't take a lot of time for the five men to become restless.

In less than an hour they decided in a change of plans. Instead of waiting for the women to finish whatever it was they were doing and come out, they would go in after them. If anyone got in their way, they would just shoot them.

Lisa picked up on their movements immediately. With her plan for them now changed, she used her quick dial on her cell phone to dial 911. When she got her answer, she rapidly explained to the operator about the armed men, and gave her the address of the beauty shop. Then she said, "A kidnapping in progress. Armed men involved."

She then yelled at the five men just rounding the back corner of the house. "Stop there, and drop your weapons. Failure to do so will get you shot." Four of the men did as they were told. The one who didn't started shooting at Lisa as soon as he turned in her direction.

Afraid his wild shots might hit some innocent person, she put a bullet in him. It wasn't a kill shot, but it did take him completely out of the action. She moved in on the four men still standing.

"Who the hell are you, and who sent you?" she demanded.

Three of the men, who were members of The Pride Guys for a year or more, refused to answer. The fourth man, who was the youngest member of the group, along with being the newest member, was too proud of that fact to stay quiet.

"We are The Pride Guys," he loudly proclaimed. "And you, Lady, are in trouble now. We will be taking care of you, and I for one, am going to enjoy ripping those clothes off you and fucking your brains out. All us Pride Guys can damn well show you what a real man is."

It was a struggle, but Lisa controlled her desire to put a bullet in his head. He'd given her most of what she wanted. The fact that they were part of The Pride Guys.

She asked the talker, "Why are you after us?"

"To get at Mack Thomas, Lady. Why the hell do you think? If we just wanted to fuck you, we coulda done that already." He'd forgotten that the gun was pointed at him. Lisa was still struggling to not tighten down the finger now pressing rather hard on the trigger of the gun in her hand. It was only her force of will that kept it steady until help arrived.

The local cops arrived first, with two sheriff's vehicles minutes behind them. Lisa called Dale directly, so he wasn't far behind them. The first cops to get there weren't sure what to make of the whole deal.

They didn't know Lisa at all, and Wanda only slightly. The sight of Kathy came more of a shock to them than anything. They knew who she was, but were surprised to see her there. How could someone so famous be mixed up in a shooting? They weren't sure either, who it was they should arrest. Lisa's story seemed to make sense to them, but she's the one who shot someone. At first they didn't think that any of the five men did any of the shooting. Lisa had to point out the wounded man's gun before they realized what happened.

The sheriff's deputies helped straighten things out, and they were the ones to initially keep all of The Pride Guys there. When Dale came, he straightened everything out in a very short time. But he still had a difficult time relating to Kathy.

She, on the other hand, purposely ignored him. She had done everything she could to apologize to him, and make it clear that she was willing to make major changes in their life. So she now considered it up to him to either accept or reject her. But she was more and more believing the acceptant part wasn't going to happen.

It was a long day, sorting things out. While that was being done, because of Lisa and Wanda's insistence, Kathy's hair was finished. When they got home, Lisa and Kathy talked about Lisa's harsh comments, and Lisa apologized for them. They were soon friends again.

After discussing The Pride Guys, with Mack and Roy, they decided on a morning meeting at breakfast, to try to find a solution to the problems they were having with them. Something they all knew would be difficult to do.

CHAPTER 26

Terrance Withers was now a proud member of The Pride Guys. He'd passed their initiation with flying colors. All he needed to do to prove his worth, was kidnap and rape the daughter of a liberal member of the Minneapolis city council. The type of task he had a lot of practice doing. He loved the moments of total control he had while doing it. It was the kind of control he had expected to have over Kathy. Control he still expected to have. All he needed was to have her where she couldn't run away. Once there, if she wouldn't totally submit to him on her own, he could always beat her into submission.

He was sure he'd get her now, with the help of his new friends. The Pride Guys. What a great group. What a great name. For Terrance, it was a wonder to hang with guys who took such awesome pride in being male. He loved the fact that they all did everything possible to shed any traces of femininity they might have had. They were true men, all the way.

Like the true men they were, they were now making plans to, one way or the other, capture every woman who was in any way connected to Mack Thomas, or Refuge Rescuers. Once they had them, the Thomas men would be easy to trap and kill.

Terrance, of course, was most anxious to grab Kathy. All parts of his body grew with his excitement when he thought about it. Almost all the men in the Northern Minnesota Chapter of The

Pride Guys, were in favor of getting their hands on Lisa first. The exceptions to them were two of their members who wanted to first go after Lisa's younger sister, Julie. They didn't consider her important in the scheme of things, since she was only a receptionist. It was her very young body they wanted.

They also hoped she would still be virgin. For them, there was nothing like taking a virgin, especially when they bled good. The sight of all that new red blood running down their legs was a super turn-on for the two. Lucky for Julie though, their request to take her first was voted down.

As much as The Pride Boys valued what they called freedom, it was actually just an unwillingness to stay organized and follow orders.

Even so, they somehow managed to keep tabs on the women they were watching. That meant they were ready to deal with them the day Kathy decided she wanted to spend all of it with her aunt, Theresa.

To do that, it meant Kathy needed to set her alarm clock. Theresa was always the first one up every morning. To spend the whole day with her, Kathy would be getting up a lot earlier than she normally did. Because Kathy would be out and about, and it still wasn't considered by any of them for it to be safe for her to do, Lisa also got up far earlier than normal. She would be with them all day, regardless of what they are doing.

Theresa didn't let it show, but she got a good internal laugh when she watched Kathy and Lisa struggle with the early hour. That small bit of personal fun stayed with her until breakfast. Even so, she carried on with her early morning chores the same as she always did.

The first one was seeing to her five pigs. They were housed in a large pen. Enough room so they could stretch their legs walking around in it. They were held in there with pig fencing, buried about a foot into the ground to prevent them digging under it to escape. Something pigs were often artists at doing. She first checked to ensure the their waterers were working properly. Next, she filled their feeders with a food Ben blended for them. Finally, she gave them a five gallon bucket of vegetables, that were culled from the previous days harvest.

Because Theresa was who and what she was, each pig insisted it needed to have her scratch their ears before she could leave their pen. They all stopped eating, for the few moments they watched her walk away. They left no doubt that they would have liked for her to stay with them longer.

"What are you going to do with the pigs?" Kathy asked her as they walked over toward the chicken pasture.

Lisa rolled her eyes at Kathy's question. How could she not know?

"We eat them," Theresa answered. "They're butchered at around two hundred pounds. We donate some of the meat to the local food shelf. But we eat most of it."

"Doesn't it bother you to do that. You treat them like they're pets. I don't think I could butcher an animal after I raised them the way you do. It would be too hard to lose them."

"The truth is, Kathy, sometimes I do make the mistake of becoming too fond of some of them. Butchering time can be kind of painful then. At the same time though, while we have the pigs, we try to give them the best life we possibly can. I don't know that it totally justifies what we do or not. But I do know that what we do is a better way than supporting the meat industry we have in this country now. The way the big corporations raise all animals goes way beyond just cruel. It's down right vicious. And only done the way it's done to make the rich man richer. Animals can be profitably raised, doing it without the cruelty used by the corporations."

"That makes a lot of sense." Kathy shook her head. "I agree with you too, that your way of raising pigs is far better than the way the corporations raise them. But I still don't think I could do it."

"You aren't alone there. Most people who care about animals can't. Almost everyone now is too far separated from the way food is produced to have any real idea about any of the immense amount of cruelty involved in raising most farm animals."

Kathy turned to Lisa. "How do you feel about it, Lisa?"

"Like Theresa, my feelings are mixed. But I was raised on a dairy farm. More often than I care to remember, we would be forced to put down an animal because of an injury or something. That makes me more than aware of the way life really is. And what really is, is the fact that we humans slaughter countless numbers of animals every year for food. And the way a huge portion of them are raised, should be against the law."

Kathy looked away from Lisa and stared at the ground. "I think I've been safely tucked away in my own little part of the world too damn long."

They were quiet then, until they came to the chicken coop. It was designed and built by a local carpenter the previous year. It was built large enough to hold a little over a hundred chickens. Currently seventy-five called it home.

Originally, when Theresa started raising chickens, they were housed in portable coops. They were kept with the cattle being raised by Roy and Wanda. But since they started the detective agency, and Roy and Wanda stopped raising cattle, the chickens were now kept in the more permanent coop.

Letting the chickens out every morning and locking them up every night were another two things Theresa did every day. The chickens spent most of every day outside. But it was necessary for them to be penned in the coop every night, after it became dark, because of predation. There was almost no end to the number of predators that favored chickens at mealtime. And nighttime was mealtime for most of them. Since roosting chickens are extremely vulnerable, it was necessary to keep them locked in a tight coop at night.

The chickens seemed to prefer the safety of the coop at night too. But every morning, when Theresa opened up the coop, she got the treat of watching them rush outside to begin their everyday celebration of life. Their joy of being free once again, to hunt and peck, was a sight to delight anyone who could appreciate the simple joy of being alive.

Their enthusiasm and antics gave Kathy a new feeling of how lucky she was to be where she was and who she was. Seventy-five critters who now seemed like little people were giving her some of the joy they were filled with. So much, that they had her laughing before they were all out of the coop. Theresa and Lisa were smiling. Something it was difficult not to do, no matter how many times a person watched a flock of free running chickens come to life on a morning filled with sunshine.

Theresa checked their waterers to be sure they were working correctly. She then checked their feeders. This morning they still had plenty of food. They ate very little commercial feed during the summer, and could have done just fine without any. Theresa gave them feed only as a supplement to their main diet. The land around them provided a more than adequate diet. It was, in fact, a much better diet that could be purchased in a bag in any feed store in the world.

They were surrounded with healthy food they loved. Green plants. All day they picked away at grass and a huge variety of broad leaf plants. It was not only filling, but loaded with nutrition too. All the green stuff also benefited the people who were privileged to eat the eggs the chickens produced. It helped fill the eggs with vital nutrition. The best thing the green provided though, was color and flavor. The yolks of an egg laid by a pastured chicken were a bright orange and contained at least twice the flavor of a store bought egg. At least twice the vitamins and minerals too.

The chickens also ate a huge variety of bugs, worms, and seeds. All foods they thoroughly enjoyed. They never traveled far from their coop, but enjoyed the traveling they did. Along the way, they frequently stopped to scratch the ground and peck away at whatever it was that they dug loose with their sharp claws. Hunting and pecking was their first love.

Kathy didn't say much about the chickens. She just rightly assumed that most of them would be allowed to live out their full lives, regardless of how long they continued to lay eggs.

The last stop was to check on the three steers that were being raised for meat. The pasture they were in could have, in a sustained way, fed at least fifteen steers. So they were on a pasture which provided more food than they could possibly eat. That meant that all Theresa needed to do was check to be sure their water tank was full.

Cattle can be terribly curious creatures though, so they insisted on checking out Kathy and Lisa. They already knew Lisa, but rarely saw her this early in the morning, so they did wonder why she was there. When Kathy stood next to the fence, one of the steers decided her blouse looked good enough to eat. It grabbed the sleeve of her blouse and proceeded to chew on it. She was again laughing as she pulled away from the curious steer. Once her arm was loose though, she did take time to give the friendly critter a few head scratches.

"It's time to get ready to make breakfast," Theresa told them then. "You guys can go back home for a while, or you can wait for me in our kitchen. I always shower before Ben and I start cooking."

"I think," Kathy said, "that a shower is a good idea. Seeing all these critters this morning was fun, but they do tend to add to whatever scent we might already have."

"I agree," Lisa said too. "We'll see you at breakfast."

Mack was up and in and out of the shower by the time they got back to their house. So Lisa was able to take her shower in the master bath right away. Kathy used the shower in the bedroom hallway. They planned to go with Theresa to the community garden after breakfast, so they dressed accordingly.

Lisa wasn't worried about Kathy visiting the community garden, but she was determined to be careful anyway. At the same time, she didn't want to make the people there who would be tending their garden plots nervous. So she used a special holster for her pistol, which she carried at the small of her back. She wore her blouse untucked, so it more or less covered her gun.

Mack couldn't help commenting on how they looked after they finished dressing and joined him in the living room. "It is nothing short of amazing," he told them, "how beautiful two women can look, wearing such ordinary clothes."

"That's enough flirting from you for the rest of the day," Lisa warned him. "You're only supposed to do that with me. Besides, Kathy's a married woman."

With a twinkle in her eye, Kathy answered Lisa's comment. "But the way things are going, it's hard to say for how long. So you're right, Lisa. Mack probably should be careful with his flirting." With that, she chuckled to herself.

Lisa managed a smile, but she carried a slight frown on the way to Ben and Theresa's for breakfast. Mack felt slightly out of balance from Kathy's comment, and decided that she was right. He should be careful with his flirting in the future. Especially since four out of the six women who were going to be eating breakfast at Ben and Theresa's this morning liked to flirt. It was their favorite way of teasing.

Julie didn't, because she considered Mack to be kind of an old man. Besides, he was married to her older sister, and the last thing she wanted to do was upset Lisa. Theresa didn't flirt with Mack because she would never consider flirting with anyone. She was deeply committed to Ben. He was her world, and it was a better world than she'd ever previously known. So she wasn't about to mess with it for something as ridiculous as flirting.

Roy and Wanda had a different track on the subject. Roy especially. For them, if it was done all in fun and not carried beyond that, it was something they often did. So when Mack walked into the house with Lisa and Kathy, he couldn't resist letting two beautiful women that he not only noticed them. He also appreciated the fact that they were in the same room as he was.

"Mack Thomas," Roy said, "It would be a great day, if I should ever be as lucky as you. Having the privilege of escorting two women as beautiful as those you just brought in with you."

Mack looked at Wanda and winked. "I don't know, Roy. While you're looking at what you don't have, I might just sneak away with what you do." He paused, looking from Wanda to Roy, then back to Wanda. "What do you think, Wanda? Are you ready to sneak away with me as soon as he's not looking."

"If he's looking at them when he is, I think that might be fun to run like hell."

Lisa was laughing, but she broke into the conversation anyway. "That's enough, Guys. If you're not all careful, it might be me and Ben who run away."

"Sorry, Lisa," Ben answered. "But my wife says I can't go nowhere until we're done with breakfast. So tell Theresa what you want, and we'll get to cooking."

Telling her what they wanted for breakfast this morning consisted or only needing to say how many eggs each of them wanted. Because Ben knew Theresa would be spending her day with Kathy and Lisa, he changed the way he prepared the meal.

To ease up on the amount of work she had to do at breakfast, he cooked the sausage and bacon ahead of time. Toast and potatoes were also cooked and loaded on platters, already on the table. A bowl of fresh fruit was in the refrigerator, waiting to be eaten at the end of the meal.

When they finished eating, Lisa, Kathy, and Wanda made another basic change in the routine. They insisted that Ben and

Theresa sit at the table and enjoy a cup of coffee. They would do the cleanup. Something that took longer than normal, given the fact that they weren't used to working together in a strange kitchen.

But they did manage to get it done. When they were ready to leave for Kingsburg, and the community garden, Mack spoke up. He didn't want to put a damper on their day, so he'd waited until now to say anything.

"I know you know what to do. But I can't help it. I have to warn you anyway. Be damn careful while you're in town. If you see anything that looks at all suspicious, come back home, call me or Dale, or if you need to, call 911. Don't try to handle whatever it is alone. I know you're all capable, but it doesn't hurt to ask for help when it's so readily available."

Lisa answered him. "We'll be careful, Mack. Wanda's driving. Theresa's riding shotgun. Kathy and I will have the back seat. We'll be watching all directions. Not only while we're driving. While we're at the garden, Wanda and I will both be watching what's happening around us. I'm armed, and so is Wanda."

"Good. You know we all want you to be able to take Kathy out like this. And have a good time without the rest of us tagging along. But we want you to be safe too."

"We know, Mack. We know. So we'll call if we need you."

Lisa knew that they could run into trouble, going the way they were. But she also knew that it would be wrong to force Kathy to be locked up like a prisoner. That could often be as bad or worse than whatever the men, The Pride Guys or Terrance Withers or whoever, might try to do to them.

A small part of Lisa also somewhat hoped Terrance Withers would show up alone, or at least without too much help. He had, directly or indirectly, been at least partly the cause of a lot of problems they were having. It was true that Kathy was partly responsible too. But she wasn't wanting to own and totally control someone the way Terrance was. Nor was she now hell bent to commit a second rape and probably a few murders. So Lisa, to a large extent, had special place in her heart where she hated Terrance Withers, and all men like him. What men like him did to her when she was still just a kid created that spot. Being kidnapped and repeatedly raped ensured that nothing was ever going to make it disappear. So getting the chance to deal with him would not be a disappointment to her.

The trip to Kingsburg seemed to go smoothly. Nothing and no vehicles they saw seemed overly suspicious. At the community garden, Lisa got out of Wanda's SUV first. She looked around, then took a quick walk through the parking area to check for anyone in any of the cars or trucks parked there. Finding nothing suspicious, she signaled to Wanda that it should be safe for them to come out.

Lisa and Wanda split apart some, to be able to watch a larger part of the garden. Kathy went with Theresa as she began her walk through the garden. As they moved along, she frequently stopped to chat with people who were there, working in their individual plots. Often as not, she answered questions. They could run from why are the leaves on my tomatoes turning brown, too is it too late to plant radishes. She was always being asked about plant varieties, with the most often question asked, "What kind of tomatoes should I plant next year? The ones I planted this year didn't do as well as I hoped."

Whatever the questions were, if she didn't know the answer, she tried to find one on the tablet she carried with her. When she started as manager of this community garden, she wasn't all that expert about gardening or using Google on a tablet. Now though, she was expert on both subjects.

Kathy knew Theresa was smart. She had to be as far as Kathy was concerned. Anything else would be unlikely, given she was her mother's sister. Linda had been more than just smart. She was wise. Something that Kathy was now seeing in her aunt.

Kathy was seeing something else too. An innate patience and kindness that went beyond what most people might share in a place like this. It really mattered to her that everyone who planted anything in one of the plots was successful. It also seemed to Kathy that her attitude and approach tended to carry over onto many of the people gardening there.

As much as anything she knew about them, or had seen them do, this garden impressed her. Without any pay, and too often with too little thanks, Theresa was spending a few hours several mornings of every week during every summer, managing this garden.

Mack and Lisa occasionally visited it, helping if they could. Most of all though, they spent a lot of money to purchase the land it was on, and they paid the too high property taxes every year. Taxes purposely too high, in the hope they would force the garden property to be sold.

Ben provided starter plants in the spring for those who couldn't afford them. When extra help was definitely needed, Roy and Wanda were often there. And finally, Sue kept track of everything that needed to be kept track of, concerning the garden.

Many of the people who used one or more of the plots, didn't know much more about the garden than the fact Theresa was the manager. But very few who were part of it, didn't appreciate the fact that they could raise at least a small part of what they ate. They loved that fact. And they could do it on clean, organic ground that was available to them for just making the effort to apply for a plot. And once they got on it was their's, without having to reapply every summer.

As Kathy moved through the garden, she saw the joy people got from their plots of vegetables and flowers they were responsible for growing. She more and more realized how fortunate she was. It was true that she worked hard from the time she was still very young to become the singer she was. But to gain the fame and fortune she had took some luck too.

That realization brought forth the memories of the night she asked Dale for a divorce. For a moment, she hated herself for what she'd done. Then she hated the man who'd been, what to her now, was a ridiculous influence on her.

And as those thoughts filled her, she saw him. Terrance Withers and one other man were just getting out of a pickup truck in the parking lot. He was watching Kathy, a huge smile on his face as he headed her way. He didn't get far. Lisa quickly moved in front of him. Wanda spotted them as she did.

"I'm going to tell you nicely once, and just once," Lisa said, her voice grim. "Get down on the ground, face down, and put your hands on top of your head." She looked at the second man. "You too."

They both laughed until Wanda stepped up close and pointed the gun in her hand at their faces. "She wasn't kidding," Wanda snarled with gritted teeth. She waved her gun at them. "And keep this on your mind. I never, ever miss."

Terrance and his friend still didn't move. They just stood there, a smirk filling their faces. Lisa turned to Kathy, who was now close by.

"Call Mack first. Then Dale."

Kathy didn't argue. She did what she was told.

Theresa, who was there now too, asked, "What are you going to do with them now, Lisa?"

Lisa, who was still looking at their smirk filled faces, decided at that moment that just turning them over to the police wasn't going to be enough. She couldn't shoot them, but she could humiliate them. And if they decided to attack her, it would give her the opportunity to hurt them some. Or even better, hurt them a lot.

Again, she told Terrance, "Lie down on the ground now."

Of course, he was way too much macho man to do what a woman told him to do. So Lisa slapped him across the face with everything she had in her. His smirk flew away, replaced with surprise as his eyes grew wide and wet. She grinned, reared back, and slapped him with her other hand.

"Ready to do as you're told yet?" She put a hand on his chest and pushed. He staggered back. "You don't lie down," she snapped at him, "and I will damn well knock you down."

Knowing now what Lisa was doing, Wanda pointed her gun at Terrance's partner. She moved her hand, signaling him to move back and away.

Terrance still stubbornly refused to do what Lisa told him to do. "Okay, that's fine with me. I really do prefer to hurt you." She suddenly reached between his legs, grabbed his privates from outside his clothes, and yanked them upward with all the strength she had in her. He screamed.

There was now a crowd around them. Most people were aware enough to know that Terrance was probably the guilty party. He also was a good size man. Lisa was not a big woman. Yet it seemed to most of them, that if there was a fight, she had a good chance of winning.

"You are not going to get away this time, rapist," she said to him. "You tried to kill my husband. You raped my friend. You are a useless piece of rotted garbage." She pushed him again. When he stumbled back, she pushed him harder, knocking him down this time.

She stood over him. If you're smart, you'll stay down. If you're stupid, which I'm sure you are, you will get up. The thing is, I won't stop you from getting up. I will, however, hurt you a lot if you do. And I'll do it with just my hands and feet. Neither of which will stop working you over until you are damn well bleeding everywhere."

She stood there, staring down at him. She hated him enough to very much want to hurt him, but decided then that it just wasn't worth it. Why get herself in trouble over something that didn't have much value. Even if he was the worst kind of trash the earth had to offer.

Terrance was watching Lisa while she watched him. He wanted, in the worst way, to get up and break her neck. But he had doubts now, about his ability to do it. He had rarely seen, in his entire life, anyone with the confidence Lisa was now showing. The look on her face told him that she didn't have the slightest doubt about what she could do to him. So he stayed on the ground. He knew that was the safest place to wait. Either for the rest of The Pride Guys who are on their way. Or the police. Which ever got there first.

Mack was the first. Then Dale. The Pride Guys just drove by when they saw the crowd and Dale's car. They weren't, as yet, ready to take on the cops. That would have to wait until they were better prepared.

Mack knew immediately when he saw the look on Lisa's face, that she was on the edge. It was every bit as obvious that the man on the ground knew it too. The look on his face was fear. All his arrogance was gone.

"He's Terrance," Lisa said to Mack before so much as a hello. "He came here after Kathy. He didn't get her."

Dale joined them then. Lisa looked at him, her face blank now. "It would be best, Dale, if you would arrest him now," she pointed at Terrance, "for the attempted murder of my husband. For the rape of your wife. And now, for the attempted kidnapping of Kathy. You better do it now, before I kill him."

She had intentionally referred to Kathy two different ways. It emphasized the fact that if he still wanted her as a wife, he'd better say so. Because if he didn't, she would only be Kathy, not his wife. Lisa walked away, feeling so tired now she found it hard to breath. She found a bench near the garden and sat down, now knowing she came dangerously close to losing it.

Mack joined her right away. He didn't say anything. He put his arm around her and held her. Soon Kathy sat down on the other side of Mack. Wanda sat next to Lisa and held her hand. Theresa kneeled in front of her. She placed a hand on Lisa's cheek.

Theresa said, "I know how hard that was for you, Lisa, but you did the right thing. He isn't worth killing. Not unless you, or one of us, can do it without going to jail."

CHAPTER 27

Dale had a lot of questions for Wanda, Kathy, and especially Lisa, but he knew they could wait. He cuffed Terrance and his partner, then asked Terrance, "Did you really think you could get away with all this? Rape and murder. Now kidnapping. You're looking at some jail time."

Terrance worked himself into the biggest bluster he could manage. "You are a dead man," he proclaimed. "You ain't never been nothing, and you ain't nothing now."

Dale wanted to ask him why he did what he did to Kathy, but because he was sure his asking the question would give Terrance a lot of satisfaction, he didn't bother.

As soon as deputies arrived, Dale put the two would be kidnappers into the back of two different cars, and went to talk to the three Thomas women and Kathy. He asked Lisa first.

"Can you tell me what happened, Lisa?"

She looked him directly in the eye. "It's simple. They came here to get Kathy. Wanda and I stopped them. I pushed the asshole around some. Then you and Mack got here. That's about it."

"What about the attempted murder charge. Where does that fit in?"

Mack answered him. "Terrance was one of the two men who attacked Kathy and I in the refuge. Both men who were here today are part of The Pride Guys. So they are not only kidnappers and murderers. They are also terrorists."

"I know, Mack. But proving that they're terrorists is difficult. Especially with all the conservative judges we have nowadays. So damn many of them don't seem to mind domestic terrorism. Not as long as it promotes their political agenda, anyway."

"That's true. so I guess we'll have to check into it. See what we can prove."

"Just be careful when you do it. Gangs like The Pride Guys can be dangerous." Dale turned away from Mack, and bent over to look closely at Kathy.

She hesitated a moment, before meeting his eyes. "It should be you, you know, who protects me. Why isn't it? Or is it over between us?" She dropped her head, tears silently rolling down her cheeks. Her voice was rough, but she managed to speak again. "Terrance, thanks to Lisa, is no longer a danger to me. So if you don't tell me otherwise damn soon, I will assume it is over. I will go back on tour. This time, I won't be back here again. I will start over somewhere else."

When she looked up at him, he knew he no longer could dwell on it. It was time to tell her how he felt. If he could find the courage to do so. He also knew that if he didn't find the courage, it would be a huge mistake, and the most stupid thing he could possibly ever do. He momentarily turned his back, trying to pull himself together.

Kathy took his movement as a sign of rejection. She stood up and said, "It looks like it's time to go home. That is, if you and Mack will still let me stay with you, Lisa. At least until I can get my tour reorganized again."

Her words hit Dale hard. He knew in that instant that he'd better act while he still could. He turned back to Kathy, shaking his head. "No. Not today." He took her in his arms and kissed her. As soon as their lips touched, he wondered what he'd been waiting for. All the love he'd always felt for her came flooding back.

He couldn't speak. All he could do was hold her. She laid her head against his chest and let the tears soak his uniform. Only these tears were from the relief and delight in knowing the worst of the nightmare was over. They were together again. There would be a lot to sort out, many changes to be made, but they were together. Beyond that, she was sure now, they could make it work.

Dale finally managed to talk. "I love you," he said, his eyes boring into hers. "I'm sorry it took me so long to tell you. I will come and get you tonight, and take you home. But now, I have to go and finish this. We don't want him walking free because someone made a mistake."

"I know, Dale. It is important what you do. So go do it. I will be there for you when you come."

He kissed her one more time, then went back to work. This time, even though he hated the man he was forced to deal with, it was with a far lighter heart than what he'd had since that horrifying night she asked for a divorce.

That was the worst of it for him. What she did after that was no longer something that could interfere with the way he felt about her. He didn't own her. She was her own person, just as he was his own person. He'd forgotten that. He promised to never allow himself to do it again. So when he watched her take Mack's hand and hold it while he took her to Wanda's car, he could only smile. That might have bothered him before. Now he knew. They were friends. It was a good thing to have friends.

He left for his office then, and spent the next couple of hours filling out the proper forms and making sure everything was in perfect order. He would get the witness statements from Lisa and the rest of them tomorrow. Other witnesses were being interviewed by his deputies.

Once he finished that paperwork, the rest of the day dragged slowly by. It quickly seemed as though it would never end. Something that was happening different for Mack.

After they all got home, it took Kathy a while to settle down. She was happy that she and Dale were going to get back together, and should have been excited about him coming to pick her up. But she was agitated about something, and it showed. In fact, it showed enough to concern Mack and Lisa. He was the one who finally asked her about it.

"I don't mean to stick my nose where it doesn't belong," he said. "So you don't have to tell me anything if you don't want to. But if you do feel up to telling me what's bothering you, maybe I or Lisa can help."

"There's nothing bothering me exactly. It's more like something I'm really curious about. I used to wonder about it some, especially when it was going on. But not like now."

"Is it something I can help with?"

"Actually, it's something only you can help me with."

"I'll do my best to help, if you'll tell me what it is."

"I'm not so sure." She looked at Lisa. "Will it bother you if I ask Mack some questions about his personal life, before he married you?"

Lisa shook her head. She was sure Kathy was about to ask about Mack and her mother, Linda. They'd had a strange affair, that seemed to be accepted by everyone who knew about it. Including Kathy's father, Dave. They were both dead now, so it was a fact that only Mack could answer her questions. Lisa was sure then, that it was best if they talked about it in private.

"I think I know what your questions are, and it is okay for you to ask them," Lisa told Kathy. "But I think it'll be better for both of you if you have that conversation just between the two of you. It'll be much easier for Mack to give you the answers you want." She left them alone on the deck where they'd been sitting, and went in the house.

Mack didn't have to wait for a question. "Yes," he said. "Linda and I were in love. But it was different. Sometimes as if the two of us together were in a different world from the one we lived in. And I have to tell you before we go any further with this, I can't explain exactly how or why it was what it was."

"How did you know I was going to ask you about my mother?"

"What else in my past life could possibly interest you, Kathy?"

She gave him sly smile. "Everything about you interests me, Mack. Maybe especially your past life. And I plan to learn a lot more about that in the future. Most of all, when we walk the refuge together. When I can hold your hand and walk close to you and not feel guilty about it."

"Why would you feel guilty about holding my hand? Friends like you and I often hold hands."

Kathy averted her eyes and blushed. "Because, Mack, I can't explain to you what it is that it is. But with you, when it's only me and you, it's as if we've gone into a different world. One where no one else can ever come into. It's not a world where we will ever forsake those we love. It's only a place where you and I can find a kind of love that almost doesn't exist anywhere. I'm not your lover, and probably never can be, but I do love you. Most of all, I want those times when I can hold your hand, while I walk the refuge with you. You give me a kind of peace, Mack, that I desperately need. That's what's been bothering me."

"I don't know why Linda and I had what we had, It was just there, and when it showed itself to us, we embraced it. We let it give us a wonderful slice of life we wouldn't have otherwise had. I think that walking in the refuge, holding your hand, will give you and I something of that on many days in the future."

"I hope so, Mack. I surely, surely do hope so."

She left the chair she was in and sat in his lap. She kissed him mightily, letting her passion show. Then she shocked him and called Lisa. "I need to tell you something," she explained.

When Lisa joined them on the deck, she also surprised Mack when she just smiled at Kathy. "I know," she said. "You two have something special. But I shouldn't worry, because you will never take it too far. I'm okay with it. But if you ever do take it too far, keep it to yourselves. It will be better if Dale or I never know about it." She went back to where ever she was before Kathy called her.

When Dale got there to pick her up, she asked Dale to sit with her and Mack and Lisa, out on the porch for a little while. She told Dale about some of the changes she wanted to make in their lives. Most of all, she told him how she was going to scale back her singing career. Dale agreed with her ideas, and talked about some of the changes he was going to make. All of them to bring them closer, and give them more time together.

Then, when it was time to leave, she said, "There is now other thing. You have to, without any jealousy of any kind, let me and Mack have some times together." She immediately picked up on the look on Dale's face. "And, damnit, not for any damn thing like you are thinking now. We are just friends, and we love you guys and each other enough to never let our friendship be anything but what it is."

"What are you saying then?" Dale asked.

"Only that sometimes we will want to do something alone, together. The biggest and best of those things will be when we walk the refuge, and we hold hands. And if it's the right day, I might kiss him. I will never cheat on you, Dale, but I do want those times with Mack."

Dale looked at Lisa. "What do you think about it? It seems like a strange thing to want."

"No, Dale, it's not. No stranger anyway, then my walking away from my husband to spend a day with you when I thought you needed me. More than that, I took you out on a date that same night. So again, no. I don't think it's strange and I think it will be a good thing for all of us. We all need different, and that's what they need. Let them have it. And who knows, there might be some days when you and I share the same kind of thing."

Dale smiled with his answer. "If that's what I need to let you have to keep you in my life, Kathy. You've got it. I just don't ever want to lose you again."

Mack didn't comment further. He stayed quiet until they started to leave. He didn't even say anything when Kathy kissed him goodby. And wasn't upset or surprised when Lisa kissed Dale, even if it did have a fair amount more in it than just goodby.

"Now this," Mack said when they were gone, "has been an interesting afternoon."

"Yes," Lisa agreed. "And now it's my turn to hold your hand." She took his hand and led him down the hall to their bedroom. She let go of his hand and started opening the buttons on her blouse. "I don't want to hold your hand right now, Mack. I don't want to be your friend either. So you better take your clothes off this instant, or I will rip them off you."

"Are you saying, Lisa, that you want to have sex with me?"

"No, damnit, I'm demanding it."

Once they were undressed, Lisa refused to wait for any foreplay. She laid down on the bed, moved her legs apart, and pulled him down and over her. Her hand was the urgent guide, and her response was strong enough lo lift him up. He was smart, and followed her lead until she exploded with an extra strong climax.

He let her ride it out, but held himself back. They lay motionless until her breathing returned to normal. Then he took charge. He started slowly, filling her until she moaned, then rolled them over. Once she was on top. she let loose again. This time he couldn't hold back.

It took a while after, before they felt up to talking. When they did, Lisa spoke first. "I needed that. It started when you and Kathy were having your private talk. I needed it then and have needed it more every minute."

"You don't have to worry, Lisa. What there is between Kathy and I will never change what you and I have. You are the best and most important thing in my life. I want and need to keep you there. When it comes down to it, you are pretty much my everything."

"Well good." She took him in her hand. "The thing is, are you going to be able prove it again?"

CHAPTER 28

He was a big man, and strong. All his life he'd been a fighter. There were few things that could make him feel as good as beating the life out of a person. Male or female, it didn't matter to him. Sometimes, when he was in one of his many dark moods, he'd find some kind of animal to beat the hell out of. Dogs liked people and always seemed to be friendly. So he enjoyed maiming and killing them the most. People who knew him called him Buster, because he was so good at busting things.

Buster was the current leader of the local chapter of The Pride Guys. He led his men with violence and hatred. Right now, he was preaching both, and aiming them at Mack and Lisa Thomas. As far as he was concerned, one or the other of them was responsible for, or at least involved in, the death or arrest of his men.

Some of his men were occasionally arrested in the past, but for the most part the charges against them were dropped. It didn't take that much intimidation to convince people to back off.

Not those two though. It seemed as though it would be near impossible to force them to drop charges. At least, they wouldn't be able to with their normal methods. This time they would have to get more radical with their ways of intimidation.

After giving it some thought for a couple of minutes, he asked his current girl friend, who knew how to turn a computer on and off, to do some research on Mack and Lisa.

Her online investigation of Mack consisted of reading an old newspaper article about him, after he got in a gunfight at the bridge over the St. Catherine river, which was near the old refuge headquarters. It happened while the original bridge was under construction. That was followed with an article about him and what happened the day that same bridge collapsed, killing several people. From those two articles, she came to the conclusion that the bridge was a place Mack dearly loved.

Now they had what they considered was a great way to get his attention. They were also convinced that all they needed to do was to blow it up. Mack would be sure then, to get down on his knees and apologize for being so difficult. After, of course, he dropped all charges against all of The Pride Guys.

What they didn't know. What they were not anywhere near intelligent enough to learn, was the fact that Mack, deep down, hated the bridge. For him, it represented all of the wrong things, all of the crimes, related to the sale of half of the original refuge years before. Whenever he saw or drove over it, all he got was bad memories.

So when the Guys blew it into oblivion one dark night, it didn't bother him personally at all. Not as far as the bridge itself was concerned. The only immediate way it had some effect, was his concern for the many people who used that county road during their commute to the cities everyday. Now their rides to work were going to be longer and slower.

He ignored the death threats that came via snail mail, email, and even directly to his cell phone. They consistently claimed he would die if he didn't drop the charges agains all of The Pride Guys. His reaction to that was to ask Dale to get the FBI involved in the bridge explosion investigation. They did, and they ruled it a terrorist attack. That put them in a position to put some heavy pressure on The Pride Guys.

Buster didn't like the pressure at all. None of the threats they made to Mack were getting anywhere. So in their own brand of what they considered genius, they decided to go hard after Lisa.

The problem they had with that though, was the fact they weren't sure how to do it. It seemed as if a successful attack on her or Mack was close to impossible. In spite of their consistent lack of ability working with Google or anything else available to them, they did figure out that Julie was Lisa's sister. From that, they learned about Julie's daily commute between the farm where she lived and the Refuge Rescuers office.

So they decided to get to Lisa via Julie. What they didn't know was the fact she was being trained by Mack, Lisa, and Paul, on Law enforcement. Because of who her teachers were, along with her self defense training, she was getting a lot of instructions on things like how to spot a tail. Be it on foot or in a vehicle.

Like Lisa, she took her lessons to heart. In doing so, she spotted the three men in the SUV the morning they followed her to work. The first thing she did during breakfast, was tell everyone about it. That was enough for Mack and Lisa. The Pride Guys didn't know it, but they had now declared war.

They called Dale and told him about it. He didn't need to be asked to help. He said he would be there that afternoon, to assist with the planning. By late afternoon, they had their plans made, and had started setting the trap they would use to do in The Pride Guys.

They knew they couldn't control everything, but they did hope to take at least one of them alive and still able to talk. If they could manage that, the FBI could be brought in. Then, if they could get one of the Guys to talk, they should be able to raid the local headquarters of The Pride Guys, and arrest all of them.

Dale had several deputies station themselves in their cars along Julie's normal route home. He then started to drive that route. He kept his speed as slow as he could without drawing too much attention to himself. He was in constant contact with Lisa, who was driving Julie's car not too far behind him. Mack was not too far behind Lisa. Dale reported everything which could be even slightly suspicious to Mack and Lisa.

The Pride Guys didn't have the slightest clue about what was waiting for them. After they followed Julie to work in the morning without any kind of incident, they were sure they could take her without any problem. They found a little used farm road that crossed the county road. that meant they could station a car on either side of it. Cars with four men in each one.

Dale had no trouble spotting them, so Lisa knew well ahead of time what was coming. When the Guys pulled their two cars out in front of Lisa, she put her car into a slide, stopping it with the passenger side facing them. She made her exit out the driver's side door. She moved quickly to the front of her car. She stopped at the front tire, so they couldn't be exactly sure where she was.

By the time she positioned herself, Dale was turned around and heading her way, his siren wailing. He purposely had it and all his flashing lights on. He was sure the Guys wouldn't be expecting him so soon, and as he hoped it would, it threw them off balance.

Mack arrived at the scene within a couple of minutes. By the time he was out of his truck and crouched down near Lisa, all of the sheriff's cars were on their way. As Dale did, they were coming with sirens wailing and lights flashing. That's when Dale used the loud speaker in his car to tell the Guys to surrender. "You have zero chance of escaping," he told them.

There were four of them on each side of the road, trying to find adequate cover. There were some bushes and other brush, but nothing that could stop a bullet. That meant they had little to no chance of escape, no matter what they did. A gun battle wasn't an option.

As a group, they knew little or nothing about going through the woods around them, and the corn fields were like an alien place. Their cars were completely blocked. So all but one of them dropped their weapons and raised their hands.

The one who didn't was Buster. When it came to a fight, he'd always won. And he was their leader, who was only with them to be sure nothing went wrong. He couldn't see how he could let his men down. He would just have to take on the damn cops on his own. He figured his chances of beating them were pretty decent. Cops were mostly lousy shots. He lifted his gun and fired at Dale. He missed and the bullet went far over Dale's head.

The gunfight ended there. Buster didn't believe cops could shoot, but he didn't know Dale's deputies. They were trained well. Each of them fired twice. None of them missed him with either shot.

Mack and Lisa didn't do any shooting. They knew that Buster didn't stand any chance if he fired his gun, and they knew it would be far simpler for Dale to do the paperwork if they weren't involved with the shooting. They were also more than tired of the seemingly constant violence and killing.

Three of The Pride Guys were more than willing to talk after the FBI were called in. By the end of the day following their capture, The FBI had everything they needed to set up a raid on the headquarters for The Pride Guys.

When Mack asked them if they wanted him and Lisa along on the raid, they were given a resounding no. Dale was treated the same way when he volunteered. None of them were saddened because they weren't going to be part of it. Then the fact that they weren't, proved to be a kind of salvation for them.

The FBI made the same mistake The Pride Guys did. They were over-confident. They were certain that the Guys would quickly surrender, once they knew they were surrounded. They didn't.

In the gunfight that followed, two agents were killed and three wounded. The Pride Guys lost six dead and eight more wounded. All of those who survived pleaded guilty and were given life sentences. They took the guilty pleas, rather than gamble on the federal death penalty.

That left Mack, Lisa, and the rest of the Refuge Rescuers, at least temporarily, free from trouble with The Pride Guys. Time would tell, they knew, whether or not some other chapter of Guys would come after them. But either way, they were determined to move on, and live their lives as normal as they possibly could.

CHAPTER 29

It was a week after the FBI shootout with The Pride Guys when Mack got a call from one of the lawyers involved in the lawsuit against the Davis Drug Company.

"I have some good news, Mack," he said, his voice bright and cheerful. "We have just learned that a cure has been found for the virus that Davis Drug has been using to kill all the dogs and cats. Whether they like it or not, we can now force them to stop the killing."

"That's awesome news," Mack answered. "Who found the cure?"

"It was a small, independent lab that was working with animal control. From the time they started working on the problem until they found a cure, only took a couple of weeks. I was told that it wasn't a particularly difficult thing to do."

"So Davis Drug killed thousands of dogs and cats for absolutely nothing."

"I sure seems like it."

"Will you be able to use that fact in they lawsuit?"

"I can't say that there's a hundred percent chance, but it's close to that."

"You said that the killing can stop now. Who's going to make sure it does?"

"I can't tell you. The police, animal control? I don't know."

"Well, okay. Lisa and I aren't fully scheduled right now, so we'll look into it."

"Sounds good, Mack. And we'll be continuing our work on the lawsuit. It's looking better every day."

Mack sent Paul out to the western part of Minnesota again, to check on the killing place there. He wanted to be sure they stopped their operation. The killing was always completely wrong. Continuing to do any more, was double that wrong.

Paul knew the instant he got there that they were still in operation. He talked his way into the office of the place and questioned the manager about why they were.

"We were never told to shut down," he explained. "We get paid according to the number of animals we test. We are still being paid. So I can't see one damn reason to stop testing. Besides, it's an important drug. That virus could get dangerous."

"It doesn't bother you to be killing dogs and cats, to test for a cure that's already been created?"

"Not really. Losing my payday, and the payday for the people who work here, that's what's important. Not some useless dogs and cats."

Paul considered arguing with the man about what was wrong with what he was doing, but knew it was hopeless. For the most part, if the people involved in this, finding a cure, scam weren't the owners who lost a beloved pet, the paycheck, money, was far and away the most important thing.

He called Mack as he walked out to his car, to tell him what he'd learned. Mack wasn't surprised. He and Lisa went through nearly the identical experience as Paul did, with the first killing place they visited. They momentarily felt stymied by the situation.

He tried everything he could to contact Chad Belldweeb, the CEO of Davis Drug. He wanted to convince him to stop, but never managed to get any kind of a response from him.

He was never going to get one either. Not if Chad had things his way. He was the person who had gotten the idea for the virus scam, and he was going to continue to work for its success. He felt that he had too. If the public ever figured out that he was responsible for creating the dangerous virus, they would be outraged. It might even cost him his twenty-five million dollar a year job.

He certainly didn't want that, when there was still a chance that his people might find a cure. Then he could complete his original plan. Given the chance, he was sure it would work. Probably without a hitch. It should. It was simple enough.

Just find the cure. Release the virus, using a variety of methods. Let a lot of dogs and cats get real sick, then sell the cure at a very high price. Chad knew that the public would gladly pay nearly any price, if it meant that they could save their precious pets. The profits would be astronomical.

So what he needed to do now, was to stop the bastards who had come up with a cure. And that shouldn't be too difficult. Just have the right people killed, and their damned lab burned to the ground. So he started making the calls to put his specialty crew to work.

There was only one problem with his plan. His secretary hated him. And she overheard part of his conversation with the leader of that crew. When she did, it scared her enough so that she backed away from his office door before going in. She returned to the mini kitchen near Chad's office.

She dumped the coffee she was bringing Chad. It was part of her normal afternoon routine, so she waited about fifteen minutes. She then poured a second cup of coffee and brought it to Chad. He was off the phone and sitting back in his chair when she went into his office. He smiled and said thank you when she put the cup down on his desk.

Shortly after she left his office, she took her personal cell phone out of her purse and went into the women's restroom.

It was empty, so she moved to a far corner of the room. She first did a search for a phone number, then dialed it. The young woman who answered her call said, "Good afternoon. You have reached Refuge Rescuers. This is Julie. How can I help you?"

With a sigh of relief, the secretary said, "I would like to make an appointment with one of your detectives. For late this afternoon. His name is Mack Thomas. I heard about him and I think he's the one who can best help me."

"Before I do that, can you tell me the reason for the appointment?"

"It's about dead dogs and cats and murder. A fire too, I think."

After that explanation, Julie didn't hesitate. "What time would you like the appointment?"

"Four-thirty would be perfect."

"Okay, four-thirty it is. Do you know where we are located?"

"I have GPS, I'll find it."

"Good. Now, if you will tell me your name, it will be helpful."

"I'd rather wait until I get there. I'm kind of scared right now." But as scared as she was, she was determined to leave work early so she could talk to Mack.

"Okay. We will be looking for you at four-thirty."

Julie contacted Mack as soon as she hung up the phone. Mack told her that he would be there on time. He needed to change some of his plans for the day, but he made sure he was back in the office by four.

Lisa was with him, but they decided that it would be best for Mack to meet the woman alone at first. Paul got back shortly after four, so he and Lisa were in a conference room when the woman got there. She was in the neighborhood of forty, still had a nice figure, and the same pretty face she had when she was twenty.

She was visibly nervous when she shook Mack's hand. He asked her, "What can I call you? You don't have to tell me your real name, if you choose not to at this time. But it will be easier if I have a name for you."

"It's Joan," she answered. "It's my real name."

"Okay, Joan," he said, and took her into a meeting room. He left the door slightly open, and they sat down. "I'm Mack, as you probably already figured out. I left the door slightly open for my safety as well as yours. In today's world, a person can't be too careful."

She blushed slightly from his explanation. "I'm not here to attack you, Mack. I'm here to see if you can help me."

"That's what we're here for. So tell me what it is you need?"

"I overheard something today I shouldn't have. Something I think you should know about. If I tell you though, I might be in trouble. I might need someone to help keep me safe. The trouble is, I can't afford to pay anyone very much to do that."

"Let's not worry too much about money yet, Joan," Mack told her. "First, tell me what it is that you heard."

"Okay, but for it to make sense, I think I have to tell you who I am, and who I work for. My name is Joan Cherry. I work for Davis Drug, My boss is Chad Belldweeb. As you probably know, he's the CEO of Davis Drug. I'm his personal secretary. I have to admit, I don't like him much. He doesn't always know where to keep his hands. He's also an all around jerk."

"Are you here because of sexual harassment?"

"No. Nothing that simple. That crap I can deal with myself. Today, I accidentally overheard part of a conversation he was having on the phone. It was about the dead dogs and cats. He's the one who thought up that whole thing, and now he has to fix it or he might be in trouble."

Mack was sure now, that this was a very important conversation, so he asked Joan, "Will it be okay with you, if two of my partners join us? I think it will be helpful if they hear what you have to say. They have been working with me on this case, and they are as concerned as I am about bringing the killing to a stop. One of them is my wife."

"I guess that should be okay." As soon as Lisa and Paul were in the room, Joan said to Lisa, "You're so young and so pretty. If I didn't know you were a private detective, I could never imagine you being one."

"That's true of a lot of people," Lisa answered. "Sometimes it helps that I look the way I do. Especially under cover. Other times, not so much."

Mack asked Joan then, about the conversation she overheard. "I'll try to tell you what I heard, but I can't guaranty that it will be completely accurate. What I heard scared the hell out of me. It still scares me. The worst part of it sounded like he was hiring someone to commit a murder. I can't tell you for an absolute certainty who he wanted murdered. But I think it was those people who have that lab where they found the cure for Chad's virus."

"You called it Chad's virus. Why?"

"He was the one who had it developed. He has been the one who has thought up all of it. I guess he thought that if he could create a way to make Davis Drug even more billions than they are already making, his job would be more secure. He might be right about that a too. Like most corporate CEOs nowadays, he isn't really all that damn good at it. The truth is, most of the work he gets credit for, I do."

"So you think he's trying to have those people murdered so he can keep the scam with the virus he started going until it finally works?"

"Yes. He wants to burn their lab down too."

"It sounds like he's getting desperate. Is he really that worried about his job?"

"I think so. He makes a good twenty-five million a year, but that's not enough. He wants even more. So losing that will really get to him."

Lisa asked Joan, "Why is it, that you came to us with this information? Why not the police?"

"I came here because I'm afraid of Chad. I think he might have me killed if he knew I told anyone about what he's been doing. And I don't believe the police could or would protect me. Also, what I read about you on Google, you already have an awful good reputation."

"That's good to hear about us. But we are limited as too how far we can go with this. If we are going to stop Chad, and the people in Davis Drug who support him, we will eventually have to get the police involved."

"I hate hearing that. I don't trust them enough to let you tell them who I am."

"I guess I can understand that," Mack explained. "But there is one man, a man I'd trust with my life in any situation. I'd like you to talk to him and tell him what you've told us. If we can get him to agree. I think we can put a stop to this, without you being directly involved."

"Good, because I think it will be punishment enough for doing the right thing when I lose my job. It doesn't pay me what I'm worth, but it'll be tough to find another one that pays as good as this one does. I don't want to get murdered over this mess too."

"We'll do our best with it," Mack promised. "And we'll definitely stay in close touch."

As she stood up from her chair to leave, Lisa asked, "Do you feel safe going back to work tomorrow?"

"More or less. Chad doesn't know I'm here or that I talked to anyone, so I should be okay. But if I start to feel too uncomfortable, I'll get the hell out of there."

"Good, and if you feel as though you need us for anything, let us know."

Joan nodded her head, then quickly lifted it and looked at Mack. "One more not so small thing. What are you going to charge me for what you're doing?"

Mack almost laughed. "Not a thing. If anything, you don't owe us, we owe you. No matter what else happens, we won't be charging you for anything. You've provided us a service, not the other way around."

Joan left then. Mack, Lisa, and Paul sat quietly for a while then, each wondering how deep they were going to get in this case now. The bad guys were still killing animals and were now planning arson and murder. They knew they would have to be careful to not get so deep they drowned.

CHAPTER 30

Mack called everyone together to tell them what he learned about the ongoing investigation into the murdered dogs and cats. When he finished telling them, Roy had a question.

"Do you really think a CEO of an international drug company would commit murder to keep a scam like this going? I know that what the company will gain if he makes it work seems like a lot of money to us. But compared to the profits Davis Drug already makes, it isn't that much. Why would he jeopardize all that?"

"I can't begin to answer that, Roy. Why would anyone, even someone broke and hungry, do what's being done for that scam? It's cruelty that goes beyond anything I can define."

"It is that," Roy agreed. "The thing is, that kind of cruelty is rather common, no matter where you look. The best example is the meat industry in this country. The way meat is raised is every bit as cruel as anything going on in the dog and cat scam. It must be that our dirt bag CEO just thinks he can get away with it. People just don't care enough about the welfare of animals. Not beyond their own pets anyway."

"I don't think that it's so much they don't care. I think it's more they don't know how to do anything to change what's going on."

Roy gave Mack a sad half smile. It looks, doesn't it," he grumbled, "like it's going to be up to us again."

Mack couldn't come up with so much as a half smile. A controlled frown was the best he could manage. "It's beginning to look like it. Anyone got an ideas?"

Paul spoke up. He started with a question. "What do we know about the people who did find the cure?"

Mack told him. "The lab is owned and operated by a couple. I don't know too much about them. He's somewhat older than she is. Like us, their home isn't far from their lab. I doubt they have any idea that their lives might be in danger because of what they accomplished."

"I agree with Roy," Paul said. "I think it is up to us to finally bring this nasty scam to an end. But the first thing we've got to do, is see to it those folks are protected. We've all seen enough, been through enough, to know that just because someone has a big time job like CEO of an international corporation, it doesn't mean they're above murder."

"I can't argue that," Mack said. "But how the hell are we going to do it. We don't have enough of anything to be able to give them protection twenty-four/seven. And that's what they need."

"There's another way to deal with it. Let's talk to them, explain what we know, then hide them somewhere. We have the perfect couple to replace them. And those two have proven that they are naturals for undercover work."

Shaking his head, Roy looked at Wanda. She nodded back at him, twice. "Okay," he said. "So how are we going to get this set up? We might not have a lot of time. That CEO, Chad Belldweeb, is probably going to be in a hurry to get rid of those people and their cure."

"I agree, Roy. I think we need to get together with Sue, and learn all we can about those people before we try to contact them."

They went over everything with Sue then, and she got busy online. After she finished with the lab people, she researched Chad and Joan, the two people running Davis Drug.

Joan came out clean. She was married, had two children. The oldest was a daughter. The son was two years younger. Her marriage appeared to be sound.

Chad Belldweeb didn't come out looking near so good. He was divorced. His ex-wife sued him for it, citing adultery as the reason. As a teenager he was locked up twice. Once for giving a boy three years younger than him a malicious beating. The record for the other time was sealed tight, but Sue manage to hack that system and get the information. He was given two years for torturing small animals. Dogs and cats were his specialty. His personality hadn't really change as he grew older. He just managed to control it, to hide it better.

Learning about his background convinced the Refuge Rescuer's crew that Chad was definitely capable of murder. Whether he committed it himself or hired it done, there was little doubt that he would go after the research lab couple. Sutra and Justin Brown needed protection. And since it was highly unlikely that any official part of society would do it, Refuge Rescuers felt like it was up to them.

They needed to contact Sutra and Justin. Something they knew would be difficult. Because of their development of the cure for the virus that had already killed so many animals, they were barraged with a large assortment of calls.

They called Dale for help. He agreed to verify their identity, if or when Sutra or Justin called him. Wanda tried many times to call them, but their phone always went to voice mail immediately. She finally gave up on that approach. Roy and Wanda decided then to take the direct approach, and drive to their lab and see if they could make a connection there. Paul went along to cover for them in case they were asked too many technical questions about police work. Roy and Wanda still had a long way to go before they could answer many questions on that subject.

They got as far as a security guard. Something they didn't expect. He was also something they didn't need. Nor did the Browns, since he proved to be rather incompetent. He took out his gun when they requested he inform the Browns that they were there. He waved the gun around, close to Roy's face.

"You all have to leave," he warned, "or I will shoot you. They don't want to talk to nobody, no how."

Roy's patience was already on a thin edge, and he hated having a loaded gun waved in is face. Especially by one who obviously didn't have the slightest idea how to handle a gun. He was a rent-a-cop from an agency that didn't bother with things like training their gun handling employees.

So Roy took the gun away from him. He handed the man his business card and a short note explaining who they were. It also gave them instructions on calling Dale, and information about the Clayborne County Sheriff's Department. He sent the man to find Sutra and Justin.

Fifteen minutes later, the man hadn't returned. They then decided one of them should go find someone they could at least talk to. Paul went, because he was the most formally dressed of the three of them. He was wearing a suit and tie. Roy and Wanda were in shirts and jeans.

When Paul entered the building, he found himself in a small reception area. The rent a cop was standing there in front of the reception desk. He was doing a good job of annoying the pretty young receptionist there.

She looked up from her desk and asked with a smile, "What can I do for you?"

Paul explained who he was and basically why he was there, but leaving out the concern about murder part. She went back to the lab and returned with Sutra about five minutes later.

As soon as they were introduced by the receptionist, she said, "I called your sheriff friend. He verified who you are. Where are the other two who are supposed to be here with you?"

"They're waiting outside. We didn't want to upset anyone by all crowding in here at once."

"Well, bring them in. Then you can tell me what this is about. I know you've come a fair distance, so it must be at least somewhat serious."

"It's real serious," Paul told her. "I'll get Roy and Wanda, and we'll fill you in on what's going on. Then, hopefully, we can do something about it."

When Paul, Roy, and Wanda finished telling Sutra and Justin what was going on and why they were there, they were left near speechless. Sutra still carried a wide eyed expression of shock when she asked, "Do you really mean to say that you want us to go into hiding? And you want to replace us? That you are willing to take the chance of maybe getting killed instead of us? Why? You don't even know us."

"To start with," Wanda answered, "it's our job. More than that, we want to catch the man responsible for the murder of so many innocent animals. And just as important, it makes no sense at all for us to stand by and let innocent people like you two get hurt or killed when we can do something to stop it."

"I just don't know about this." Sutra turned to her husband, Justin. "What do you think about it all? Should we let them do what they want, or should we be the bait for whoever wants to get us?"

Paul interrupted them. "Before you answer her, Justin," he instructed him, "listen to what I've got to say." Paul paused and took a couple of deep breaths. "I'm pretty sure that both of you are thinking now, that it will be cowardly for you to let someone else take your place, just because what's going to happen is dangerous. Nothing could be farther from the truth. It actually takes more courage to walk away in a situation like this, than it does to stay. But doing it, you could very well be responsible for saving innocent lives. Above and beyond yours.

"You will also increase the chances that we will be able to take one or more of the people who come here alive. Doing that will almost ensure that we'll be able to get the proof we need to arrest and convict Chad Belldweeb."

"I don't know," Justin said. "I feel like I'm shirking my duty, if I hide just because it might get dangerous."

"I know. But what I'm telling you is that you're not. Your duty, first and foremost, is to protect your wife. You can do that if you keep her out of the line of fire. You have to remember, we are far better equipped to deal with any shooting. All three of us are well trained with weapons of all types, and shoot expert at the firing rang. But Wanda here is exceptional. When she shoots at something, she never misses. She comes as close to perfection as it's possible to come. And that's something you can't do if you stay here."

"I guess you're right," Justin agreed. "But if there's anything else we can do, we will be more than happy to do it."

"I'm sure," Paul said, "we'll find plenty for you to do before all of this is finished."

CHAPTER 31

Chad Belldweeb was considered by many to be brilliant. He was CEO of one of the richest drug producing corporations in the world. And he'd managed to rise that far in the ranks with only a four year degree in business. And that was from a small college located in his home town.

What few people knew, was the amount of backstabbing and other nasty things he'd done to get where he was. When it came to that, he was very much like Donald Trump. No amount of lies, cheating, fraud, and outright terrorism was too much for him to do, if it advanced his own interests.

At the same time, he was often stupid. As is Donald Trump. And when it came to utilizing his, what he called, specialty team, he could be sloppy and careless. He was also over confident about their abilities. In this particular venture he was sending them on, he was also underestimating the opposition. It was true that he didn't know that Joan, his private secretary had informed on him, but he made no effort to check anything beyond the addresses of the lab and the people he wanted destroyed. He also saw no reason to send a large specialty team to do the job. So he only requested that two men be sent to do it.

The lead man of the two was big, slightly overweight and just a bit out of shape. He was veteran of a street gang that specialized in robbing all night service stations and raping underage girls.

His partner was an ex-boxer, who was never quite up to par in the ring. He had a lot of fights and got hit in the head a lot. Of the near thirty he fought, he won three and was knocked out ten times. He was no longer the most rapid thinker around.

They wanted to burn the lab first. For them, there were few things that could bring joy to their hearts quite like watching someone's building burn to the ground. If there was someone inside, screaming from the horror of burning alive, so much the better.

But even they, with their limited abilities, especially the ones that involved thinking, could figure out that burning the lab first might give Sutra and Justin some warning. So they decided to kill them first. They decided to do it the same night Roy and Wanda replaced them in their home.

In a lot of ways, the team did Roy and Wanda a favor but doing it so soon. Instead of becoming dull from spending too many nights waiting for something to happen, Roy and Wanda were suffering from the first night undercover jitters. It kept both of them wide awake late into the night, so when the attack came, they were as ready as they possibly could be for it.

After the two men stalked the house, they decided that it only made sense to go in through the patio door in the back of the house. Roy left it partially open intentionally, as an invitation for them. It was far easier for him to stop someone who was breaking in, if he knew ahead of time where they would be doing it.

Wanda was watching the front of the house when they tried to sneak in through the open door. Roy heard them coming, and was waiting for them. When the first man, the boxer, stepped in, Roy was ready for him. He quickly stepped behind the man and hit him on the back of the head. Just the way it's done in the movies. It knocked him down, but not out.

Before Roy could finish him, the veteran charged into the room. No lights were on, so he had trouble focusing on Roy, and therefore missed him when he shot at him. Roy dove off to one side to avoid the second shot fired, but landed on his gun hand and lost the gun.

He heard Wanda rush into the room as he tried to roll away from the veteran. He heard a crash as Wanda ran into an unseen coffee table. The boxer made it to his feet and managed to knock her down. She twisted around as she fell though, and landed far enough away from the boxer's foot, flying at her face, so it missed her. As he moved closer, intent on trying another kick, she raised her gun.

"You don't want to do that," she told him. "If you don't back off and drop your gun, I'm going to shoot your nuts off."

The boxer didn't believe her, so when he tried another kick, she shot him. She intentionally put the bullet in his leg to warn him. If possible, she wanted to keep him healthy enough to question.

He thought she missed when the bullet hit his leg, but it hit him close enough to convince him not to gamble his manhood any further. He did as he was told.

In those few seconds Wanda was dealing with the boxer, Roy managed to regain his feet. He was far faster than the veteran, so he was able to escape another gunshot and get close enough to him to land a few blows on the Veteran's soft stomach.

But the big man was tough, despite the fact that he was in rather poor condition. Roy somehow was able to knock the gun from the veteran's hand, but several blows to the body and head still hadn't taken him out.

Wanda wanted to shoot the man, but didn't want to fire while they were bouncing around, trying to knock each other senseless. Finally, she got tired of watching them struggle. She was worried about Roy, despite the fact he was landing six or eight blows to the man's one.

In exasperation then, Wanda yelled, "Goddamnit, Roy, duck!"

He did, and then the veteran fell. His leg wound bleeding profusely. Wanda picked another leg. She figured that having two hitmen talking was better than only one. There were no vital organs in the leg.

Roy and Wanda carried zip tie handcuffs, which they used on the would be assassins. While Roy called 911 to report the break-in and shootings, Wanda put tourniquets on their legs to stop the bleeding. They then stepped back and waited for the police.

The local police arrived first. The young patrolman was somewhat overcome to find two wounded men, cuffed and with bullets in their legs. It took him a few minute to decide what to do. When he finally did, he called the police chief. A man who was exceedingly unhappy about being awakened at that hour of the night. He in turn, called the state police. They arrived promptly about an hour later.

They debated for a while as to whether they should arrest Wanda for violating the city ordinance against the use of any firearm within the city limits. After they decided not to arrest her, they finally listened to Roy's explanation as to the reason he and Wanda were there in place of Sutra and Justin Brown.

When the lead man for the state patrol learned that they were there because they were involved in trying to solve the deaths of the dogs and cats, he ordered their release. His son lost the ten year old dog he grew up with, and was heart broken about it. That meant he was anxious to let them move on with their investigation.

Mack and Lisa arrived a short time later and they all went to the hospital to question the wounded killers. Mack, along with Wanda, questioned the veteran. Lisa and Roy questioned the boxer. They split up Roy and Wanda during that process, so they would have the opportunity to work with Mack and Lisa.

They both had a lot more experience than Roy and Wanda, so it was training exercise too.

Getting the answers they wanted from the questioning of the two failed assassins proved to be a simple, easy affair. After promising the two men they would try to get them lighter sentences after they pleaded guilty, the answers came quickly.

Now that they had law enforcement personnel as witnesses, and both sessions of questions and answers recorded, that evidence along with all the other evidence they had was enough to do what it took to shut down all the killing centers.

All that was left to do about the slaughter of so many dogs and cats was to go after Davis Drug and Chad Belldweeb. That would be up to the lawyers now. Refuge Rescuers had done their part in solving the mystery.

CHAPTER 32

Mack finished pushing his reel type mower through the small piece of grass they called a lawn. He looked at Lisa, who was lounging on the wood deck attached to the back of their house.

"I don't think I'll be doing that too many more times this year," he said to her. "There's not that much of summer left."

"I know," she agreed. "Won't be long and it'll be freezing cold and we'll be buried in ten feet of snow. I'm going to miss sitting out on this deck."

"Me too. Come winter, I even miss mowing grass. Maybe we should start spending our winters in Tucson, or someplace like it."

"I think I'd like that. Trouble is, we're always working. It seems like we always have some kind of serious problem to solve."

"It's slower than usual now though. Maybe we should take a day and just kick back and not do anything too responsible."

"I'd kind of like that, Mack. Maybe have some company. Maybe cook up a barbecue?"

"We could do that. How many people would you like to have?"

"Just a few. I think it would be good to have Dale and Kathy. They need to get out and mingle. They've had a rough summer."

"Anyone else, Lisa?"

"Everybody here. Ben and Theresa, Roy and Wanda, and Sue of course. Paul and his wife for sure. If all of them come, we should ask Julie too. And if we ask my sister, we should ask my brother Ricky. And if we ask them, we should invite my folks. They won't be able to stay late because of the milking, but I know they'll want to come."

"Who else? There must be a lot more people you'd like to have here."

Lisa laughed. "I know, Mack. That's a lot more than just a few people. But how could we invite any of them without inviting all of them. They're all important to us."

"You're right. We can't have a party with only some of them. Odds are, there will be more. So let's do it next Saturday, weather permitting."

"Okay, but if we're going to have that many people, what are we going to provide in the way of food?"

"Just the basics. Theresa can make her awesome potato salad. She's got plenty of eggs from her chickens right now, so she can make it the way she always does. Double the eggs anyone else uses. You can make the coleslaw. And we can trade off on the cooking of the hot dog, burgers, and ribs. If you don't feel like making your sauce for them, we'll use something out of a bottle. We'll chop up plenty of dad's onions, peppers, and tomatoes, and let everyone put together their own hotdogs and burgers. All the buns will be store bought. If you want more, someone could make either barbecue beans or chili. Think that'll be enough."

"That should be enough, Mack."

"Good, and if we have some leftovers, it'll save you and I from cooking a few meals. That's always a treat on some of the long days we put in."

"It is that. When should we start inviting people?"

"In an hour or so. First, I want to take a shower."

"A shower? To call people? Why""

"Because after my shower, I have a date."

"Really. What if she's not willing?"

"Then I'll be heart broken."

Mack's heart stayed whole, and before the day was over, they had started what they hoped would turn out to be a great party. By then, they knew that what they would need most was good weather.

That's exactly what they got. Weather better than good. It was near perfect. The day started in the high sixties, rose to the midseventies, and stayed there. A light breeze kept the temperature moderate, whether in the sun or shade. It held the bugs to a minimum too. The sky was a bright, yet deep blue, with only an occasional wispy white cloud floating through it.

They wanted to make full use of the day light during the shorter, late summer days, so they started early. The first people to arrive were Dale and Kathy, surprising Mack and Lisa. They were the only people invited who hadn't committed to coming to the party.

Dale was all smiles when he shook Mack's hand. "I have to tell you, Mack," he said. "I think this barbecue idea you and Lisa came up with is great. After what we've all gone though this summer, this is the kind of thing we all need."

"That's why we thought it up. And I have to tell you, seeing you and Kathy here together makes all the effort it took to put together worth it."

Kathy gave Lisa hug and told her thank you for inviting them. Then she turned to Mack. Without a word, she wrapped her arms around his neck, pulled him down to her and kissed him.

When Mack pulled away from her, a confused look on his face, Kathy laughed. "It's okay, Mack. Dale knew I was going to do that. It was for you being our friend, for your understanding. I would have kissed Lisa too, but she's a girl."

"I liked the kiss," Mack said, "but you don't have to do anything special for me. I sure didn't do anything special for you or Dale."

"The thing is, Mack," Dale told him, "you did a lot. You and Lisa both. But that's enough of that for today. Except for the kissing. As long as you and Kathy don't go any farther than kissing and holding hands, it's okay with me. And I promise, Lisa and I will hold it down to that too."

People arrived steadily then. The food was served and plates were filled. Ben took charge of the grills, so the meat was cooked to near perfection. All the side dishes were greatly appreciated too. Including Mack's barbecue beans that he hastily put together the night before.'

They rented a portable dance floor, so there was a steady stream of people dancing to the recorded music being played over speakers set up in an out of the way place.

After a couple of hours, Kathy surprised everyone when she put on a recording of her music. It was all instrumental. She hooked up a microphone to the speakers and start to sing. Her voice was soft, and lightly tentative when she started, but by the third song she was putting all she had into it.

Mack decided to dance with Lisa then, but when he looked around for her, she was dancing with Dale. He wondered for just a moment if he should ask her to dance with the next song, but decided against it. They were enjoying it, and they'd all agreed. Things like dancing with the other wife was okay.

He danced a couple of dances with Wanda then. But on the third song, Roy cut in. He thought about asking Theresa, but as she always did, she was busying herself serving beverages to other people. Sue was already dancing with a man he didn't know. That was when he noticed that Beth Anderson, who was married to Bob Anderson, Lisa's father.

Mack and Beth had a history, so he wasn't sure about asking her to dance. Curiosity as to whether she would actually dance with him won out though, so he asked her.

Her answer was a big smile and, "I'd love to, Mack."

Their first song was slow, and Beth wasn't all shy about moving up close. It was followed by two more slow songs, and she stayed close for both of them. When they are followed by a fast rock and roll song, she bowed out. But she did it with a thank you and a surprising comment.

"Thank you so much for that, Mack," she told him. "It felt so very good to have your arms around me one more time. I've missed that." She walked away. Mack didn't get another chance to get close enough to talk to her again, let alone have another dance.

Lisa and Dale took a break then too, and joined Mack. Kathy was singing again, so before either one of them could say anything, he put a finger to his lips, telling them to stay quiet while she was singing. They stayed with Mack for a couple of songs, but when Kathy sang an old time rock song they both liked, they went back out on the dance floor.

Kathy sang another fast song, then changed the mood completely. The next song was an intimate love song. The kind of song she might have held on too Dale to sing it to him.

At the same time, Lisa wanted to dance with Mack to that song, so she left Dale to take him out on the dance floor. Kathy, however, decided that since Dale appeared to be busy with Lisa when she started the song, she would sing it to Mack. She moved through the people between her and Mack, and went directly to him. She took his hand and pulled him to his feet, then held him close as she sang the song directly to him and for him.

She lowered he microphone when the song was done, and as she did when she and Dale first arrived, she wrapped her arms around him and kissed him. No one would ever mistake it for a friendly kiss. There was an audible sigh from nearly everyone there when they separated.

Kathy gave them about thirty minutes more, then stopped singing. Her last song was another love song, and this time she held Dale while she sang it. He received a kiss at the end too. It had almost as much passion in it as the one she'd given Mack. The applause she got then was as enthusiastic as any she'd ever gotten. Everyone knew that they'd been given a rare treat.

For the rest of the day, Mack and Lisa mingled among the people there. They danced a few times to the recorded music, and a few times with other people. When Mack danced to slow songs with Kathy, she made sure there wasn't any space between their bodies.

When the afternoon moved into evening, the crowd steadily thinned. As it did, Mack joined in with Theresa and Ben doing the cleanup. Lisa concentrated on being a good hostess. She moved from group to group and person to person.

Then, the cleanup was done and the left over food put away. Ben and Theresa said goodnight and left. Only Mack, Lisa, Kathy, and Dale were still there. It was a day free of alcohol, so Mack opened a beer for him and Dale. Lisa and Kathy each drank a glass of wine.

"I have to tell you guys," Dale said, "you did put on one hell of a party."

"I think it came out pretty good," Lisa agreed. "Don't you, Mack?"

"Yeah. I thought it was a good party."

"Kathy?"

"It was great. It was fun singing for people I know. It's different from a huge crowd of strangers. More personal."

"It sure was," Dale said, a sly grin on his lips. "Especially that love song."

"Which one?"

"Mack's. The one you sang for Mack. Now that was personal."

"Dale, I hope you aren't going to make that into something it wasn't, and ruin what's been a really good day so far."

Dale sat up in his chair. Her comment was totally unexpected. He hoped he could convince her that he didn't mean anything negative about it. "I'm sorry, Kathy, if I said that wrong. I wasn't complaining. When you sang it to him the way you did, it was romantic. But in a nice way. It wasn't like you were about to do something you shouldn't. It was much more just you showing that you could really care about someone who was important to you. That's the way I took it anyway. Besides, how could I complain, after all the times Lisa and I danced."

"It's sad sometimes, isn't it," Lisa said, "how we so often misunderstand each other. It's too bad we all have to be so damn uptight about our feelings. I wonder sometimes, about the idea that you can only love, or be in love, with one person."

"It is too bad we're that way," Kathy said. "I'm beginning to understand my parents better all the time. I've never seen two people who loved each other more than those two. Yet they were so open with each other and what they did. For them, something like a romantic kiss with someone of the opposite sex who you liked, was perfectly natural. And sometimes it was okay if it went farther. You, Mack, of all people, should know that."

"I do. But I'm not sure I want to talk about it right now. After all that we've gone through this summer, this might not be a good time. There might never be a good time. It's probably best to just forget about what happened between Linda and me."

"If you're worried about me," Lisa said, "or how I might react to it if you guys talk about it, don't. I'm not going to get upset. It was a long time ago, and it hasn't hurt what you and I have, Mack. I just hope nothing ever does."

"It won't if we don't let it. Like I told you before, you are my life. Without you, nothing makes sense."

"And that's the way it's supposed to be, Lisa. Dale and I had that before I screwed up so bad. We're trying to get it back, but it ain't easy."

"The truth is though, Kathy," Dale said, "everything considered, we've come a long way. I think today proved that. There was no getting upset when I danced with Lisa too much.

And best of all, I didn't behave like an idiot when you gave Mack those kisses. The one when we got here, and the one with the song."

"I know, Dale." Kathy gave them a knowing smile. "So I am going to give all of us a test, to see if we can be who we say we want to be." She left her chair and sat in Mack's lap. "Your turn Lisa." Knowing what Kathy was trying to prove, she moved to Dale's lap. "Now," Kathy giggled, "for the next ten minutes, we are going to do some necking. No touching allowed, but a lot of honest kissing is on the menu."

She kissed Mack. His response was immediate. Soon their tongues were playing their own games. Neither Mack nor Kathy noticed, but Dale and Lisa were doing the same thing. They were all feeling the affects of what they were doing, but they didn't move any further than the necking. Then Kathy moved slightly. Just enough so Dale and Lisa couldn't see the front of her body. She took Mack's hand and placed it over her breast. He moved his head back from her's. He made eye contact and gave her breast a light squeeze.

He said, "You are awesome, but no. Not tonight. Someday? Maybe?" With that he gave her the last kiss for the night.

Kathy said, "Okay. Waiting is part of life."

Lisa quickly moved over to Mack's lap. "I think," she told Kathy, "that we all just got a good lesson. What we just did was a dangerous thing to do. And we'd all better think about our partners, and talk to our partners, before we ever do anything like that again. Now it's time for you guys to go home. I hope that when you get there, you will do the same thing we'll be doing shortly after you are gone."

Dale and Kathy laughed, then stood up. Just as they did to start the day, they kissed, hugged and shook hands. Then they were in their car and on their way home.

Lisa looked at Mack. "I don't know what you thought about what happened. But I'm not at all sure that we should have done it."

"Did it bother you a lot?"

"I depends on what you mean by bother. It didn't upset me, as in I was worried about what you and Kathy were doing. It also didn't upset me because I feel guilty about it. I don't."

"Why are you upset then?"

"Because I'm not upset. It seems like I should be. It was nice. If we do that kind of thing too much, it could get way beyond nice. I don't know that it would be at all good if it did. What about you? What do you think about it?"

"It was nice. I should in some way be upset about it. I'm not. And you are absolutely correct. It was a dangerous thing to do. We'd better think carefully before we ever do it again. But I still want to be able to be friends with Kathy. Especially when it comes to things like walking the refuge with her. She wants to learn as much about it as she can. I really enjoy teaching her. That has every bit as much to do with my wanting to walk with her as the fact that I enjoy her company. Will you be okay with that?"

"Of course. Just like you are going to be okay with my helping Dale out in the sheriff's office. It's getting disorganized again, so I'm going to help him fix it."

"That's fine with me. We all need time with more than one person."

"Good. Now let's go to bed. I'm horny as hell. I've been thinking all day what I want to do to you tonight."

"Even when you were kissing Dale?"

"It was a stronger feeling when I was kissing Dale. So strong, I put his hand on my breast near the end. I hope you're not going to divorce me for that now."

"No way. Kathy did the same thing. That's why I agree with you. What we did was dangerous."

"It was, so let's go to bed and take care of what that danger contributed to. Let's make love like the world might end tomorrow."

Mack took Lisa in his arms, pulled her tight to him. He kissed her. She returned it. "No matter whatever happens, whatever dangers we face or take part in, I will always love you. You can never leave me, no matter what happens if life gets too dangerous."

Mack expected when they got into bed, that Lisa would react as she often did. It would be a wild ride. She didn't and it wasn't. They made quiet, slow love. She wanted him on top, and she pulled him tight so she could feel the full weight of him.

They took a lot of time to reach their climax. She went first. After she did, he wasn't able to hold back. It was strong for both of them, and when he moved off her, she kissed him with all the love she had in her. They held each other, knowing as they drifted off to sleep that the one they were holding was the one who they were meant to spend a lifetime with. However long that life might be.

EPILOGUE

The board of directors for Davis Drug fired Chad Belldweeb the day after the killing centers were shut down. When the police went to arrest him, they found his body inside his home office. He had been strangled, and the rope was still around his neck. A note was attached to his shirt. It said, "We were here." It was signed, Lassie and Sylvester.

The big question, when his murder was reported on the news was, "Who are Lassie and Sylvester?"

~⁘~

Davis Drug and its lawyers knew they had little chance in winning the court battle, when the class action lawsuit came close to its court date. They also knew that any more publicity about it would not be a good thing. So they opted to settle.

The settlement figure was in the billions, with several millions set aside from their fees, by the lawyers, for the people who were responsible for the investigations that made the law suit possible.

At Mack and Lisa's insistence, Dan Tucker received the highest reward for his services. He was the first to realize that someone should investigate the reason for all the dead dogs and cats.

When he got his million dollar finders fee, the thing he planned to do first was quit his job. Like most people did, he tended to look down on himself for doing such a lowly job as working in a dump. But after he gave it a lot of thought, he realized how far from the truth that idea was. The job paid a living wage and the hours were decent.

Most importantly though, the work was needed to keep American society moving on. The way the people of his country lived, having a place where their garbage could be safely stored was critical. So he continued working at the dump, knowing that when all was said and done, what he did had far more value to society than what any ten CEO Chad Belldweebs types ever contributed. So now he not only continued to work at the dump. He started everyday with a new sense of pride. In himself, and in what he did.

Refuge Rescuers was paid close to two million. After some discussion about what to do with the money, it was decided that they would keep enough of it to cover all their related expenses, including salaries. All the rest went to various charities. Some environmental, and the rest to various animal rescue organizations.

Kathy began to do what she could to restore her singing career. It was somewhat difficult, because she refused to ever again dedicate herself to it to the expense of everything in her life. That meant she didn't pick up her tour the way her management expected her to. Instead, she did as many of the previously scheduled concerts as she reasonably could. But when she did one, she flew to the city two days ahead of it. That gave her a full day of rehearsal before the concert. She always flew home the day after.

For the cities she missed, she insisted that all ticket holders be reimbursed for the ticket. But she told them to hold on to the tickets. She then rescheduled the concert somewhere in the future. It would be free for the ticket holders of the canceled concert.

Contrary to what she was told, her fans didn't hate her for what she was doing. Instead, enough of them understood her need for a change in her life style, so that her fan base actually grew.

⌒

With Kathy's new approach to her singing career, she now could find the time to do things like going out to eat. Frequently, they went with Mack and Lisa. It was something they all enjoyed, and their friendship continued to grow as they spent more time together.

It was a Saturday night, when they got together at a local restaurant. It seemed different this night though. To Mack and Lisa, Dale and Kathy seemed somewhat edgy. It was enough to concern Mack and Lisa. Was something wrong between them. After all that happened the previous summer, they worried that anything was possible.

For Kathy and Dale, there was nothing wrong between them. What was wrong, was that they want to ask Mack and Lisa a favor, and were afraid that if the did, they would be over stepping their friendship.

It didn't take long for Lisa to speak up. "Okay, guys, what's up. It's obvious that something's bothering you two, and it's driving me crazy. So it would be nice if you would tell us now, before we order any food and then find out we can't eat."

Kathy and Dale exchanged a long look. Then Dale answered Lisa's question. "We have a big favor we want to ask you, and we aren't sure we should."

"Well hell, Dale, you don't have to feel that way. If there's anything we can do to help you, I can't think of anything we wouldn't do for you."

"The problem is, the favor we want will affect more people than just the four of us."

"Who could that be?"

"Ben and Theresa and Roy and Wanda and even Sue."

"What could you want that could affect them?"

"Land. Kathy and I would like to buy five or ten acres from you. We love that open spot on the other side of the meadow at the back of your house."

"I'm sure we can sell it to you, but what are you going to do with it."

Kathy answered this time. "We want to build a house and live there. I also want to build a small recording studio. I think I can make better music in surroundings like that."

"And we very much want to downsize," Dale added. "There's no way we need a house the size of the one we live in now."

Mack smiled before answering them. When he did, it was short. "When do you want to start building?"

They had a very pleasant meal that night. At the end of it, when it was time to part and go home, Mack and Dale both received generous kisses goodnight. Generous enough to tell stories.

⟿⟾

As they often did, Mack and Lisa took an early morning ride. They drove around what was still called the Clayborne County Wildlife Refuge, even though it was now privately owned. The ride took them to the bridge The Pride Guys blew up. Mack stopped, and they got out of the pickup. Without any talking, they leaned against the truck and looked at the remnants of the bridge that rose above the flowing river.

The debris left from the explosion was gone, cleaned up by the latest out of town construction crew hired to rebuild the bridge. Much of their huge and powerful equipment was already onsite. Mack hated what he saw.

For him, the only good thing that could happen to the bridge would be the removal of every trace of it. It only held bad memories. It was on the edge of the place where the destruction of half of the original refuge began. Two young boys were murdered there. Mack and Lisa were in a gun battle there. It was a first for Mack, and this was where he killed the first man. Lisa was still a kid when it happened, but still had vivid memories of it..

For Mack, this bridge, by its very existence, represented an incredible number of things he considered wrong. So the simple act of looking at it caused him to tense up. Lisa sensed this, and took his hand in hers.

"We survived that day," she said. "We've made it through a lot of them since, and we'll make it through a lot more in the future. When I look at that horror over there, I remember how much I wanted you. I know, I was just a kid. But I knew what I wanted." She squeezed his hand. "And I'm so damned grateful that now I have it. So don't look so glum, Mack. In spite of that beast over there, you and I still have too much to ever be anything but happy about our own lives."

He didn't answer. Instead, he took her in his arms and kissed her. How could he possibly argue with her, when she was so right.

↬↫

They were out again, doing their now once a month walk in the refuge. As she always did, Kathy took Macks hand as soon as they started down the trail. And as always, she moved close to him.

"I know," she said, "that these walks are supposed to be me learning

about this refuge. But today, will you please finally tell me about you and mom?"

"There isn't that much to tell. We had some really strong feelings for each other. There was love. A lot of love actually. But we also had some kind of cosmic connection. Like the universe made a mistake, and we belonged together in another time and place. We never considered trying to be together in this world. That never would have worked. I had my life and she was madly in love with your dad."

"But you had a love affair. Didn't you feel like you were cheating?"

"I guess, according to most peoples standards we were. But we never felt like it. And your dad never objected to what we had. I'm pretty sure he thought it was special."

"What about your age difference? Didn't it bother you that she was so much older than you?"

Mack gat a chuckle from that question. "If you remember, Linda never lost the figure of the young woman she once was. She was also still a very vigorous person? And more often than you might believe, given her awesome spirit, I often felt older than her, not younger."

"Do those feeling include when you were in bed?"

"You're getting kind of personal, Kathy."

"I know. I want to get personal. I'm Linda's daughter. Sometimes I wish I could be just like her. Sometimes, I wish I could replace her. Most of the time I dream about you and I having exactly what you and mom had in that other life, in this, right now, life."

"Why do you want to do that? Isn't what you have with Dale enough? You two have a hell of a lot going for you. Some of the things that he can give you, I can't.'"

She pulled him down and kissed him. "That's the way I most want to be her, Mack. There's something about the way you always seem to understand when I need understanding. Other times you just make me feel more alive, more free, and most of all, more filled with a joy for life than at any other time."

"But you know we can't be that. We have promises to keep. And I don't think you want to lose Dale, any more than I want to lose Lisa, Only because we broke those promises. Even if you do much the same to me as you say I do to you."

"You're right. We can't do that. Not now. But you have to remember, Mack, nothing lasts forever. Not even promises. But you're right about there being a problem. I do love Dale about as much as I could ever love anyone. Even so, there's still something missing. That missing thing always appears when I'm with you. Like I said, you somehow set me free, Mack. You never come at me with a lot of expectations. It's always, whatever is, is. You were the first to really forgive me after the horrible things I did to Dale. You did that so far ahead of him. Because of that, I see almost everything about that part of life differently. I don't ever want to cheat on Dale, because I for an absolute certainty don't ever want to hurt him again. But because of what you did, of who you are, I feel more free when I'm with you than I do any other time. More even, than when I'm alone. What I really want, is to be free enough to share whoever and whatever I am with you, without it being thought of or treated like a hurting thing."

Mack finally answered her. "If it were a perfect world, that's the way it would be for all four of us. Unfortunately, it's not. I guess you and I will just have to bear with, and be damn glad we have as much as we have. For me, there's no other choice. I love Lisa too much to try to change what is."

"I know that, Mack. But we do have today, and I can still hold your hand. That will make the dreams easier." She kissed him again, took his hand, and they resumed their walk.

For the rest of the day it was filled with wild things. Critters, flowers, trees and things…"

⌇

They were in bed for the night. "Was it a good walk today?" Lisa asked.

'It was. We saw a couple of otters again. It's always a treat to watch their antics. They do love to play."

"Did she kiss you?"

"She always does.'

"Did you like it?"

"I always do."

"More than mine?"

"Nothing on this green earth is more than yours, Lisa. I love every part and parcel of you. More than anything else in my life. Your kisses are the sweetest, your body the greatest, and your love the most sacred of everything else in existence. And making love to you is like rolling around in heaven."

Lisa laughed. "I love it, Mack," she said, her voice barely above a whisper, "when you get poetic and exaggerate things about me. It takes away my doubts about me."

"Why would you have doubts about you. You are easily the most beautiful woman I've ever known. Add to that you're intelligent, independent, and strong. As far as you being my wife goes, I could look around the whole damn world, and I couldn't do better than you. And of all the men who have ever so much as seen you, they are all jealous of me because you are my wife."

"Does it ever bother you though, what happened to me when I was kidnapped. The way I was used. Sometimes I think it should turn you off. Kathy's never been used that way."

"That's never been something I've even remotely considered. What made you think I could feel that way?"

"Comparing myself to Kathy."

"Don't do that. For me, you are the best, and still the most perfect woman there ever could be. The truth is, no one else can compare."

"I love you, Mack. Now hold me. Take away my doubts, and all those things I'm afraid of."

He did, and as they held each other, she did for him exactly what she asked him to do for her.

⁓

The grass was already up to their ankles, And a dark, vivid green. Everywhere, springs wild flowers sparkled. Some were tight to the ground and others grew tall. But the most predominate of them followed the grass, giving the impression of floating in it.

As was becoming a custom, the normal way of doing things. Mack held Lisa's hand as the walked through this refuge. This small, wild place almost hidden from the trials of day to day life.

For most, it would be looked at as just some woods. For them, as they let the abundant life around them fill their senses, it was their own small, but wondrous magic kingdom and refuge.

As they walked, they stopped often to bend down to look closely at a new flower, or maybe to watch a lizard hunt one of the endless number of flying insects.

They continued to move slowly, but eventually reached the far side of the meadow they claimed for their own when the four hundred acres they shared became their's and their families.

Not too far outside the meadow, they reached a new structure. The home of Dale and Kathy. They waited on the deck built onto the back of their recently completed new home.

"Come on, Guys," Lisa called. She waved at them. "Come and walk with us. You're settled in your house now, so you have time. You have to see the treasure where you live."

Dale and Kathy joined them. She took his hand, and they moved out into the meadow.

"This is what we get to see every spring," Mack told them. "When walking this, our own private refuge, if you're quiet, you will see all kinds of critters. This is where Lisa and I first saw the bear who was around a while back."

Kathy looked around. "You know what, Mack? Sometimes, we can walk out here, and you can teach me here. Can't you?"

"Sure."

"We are all really lucky, you know," Lisa said. She let go of Mack and lifted her arm. Pointing a finger, she slowly turned in a circle. "To have all this, our own refuge. And now friends to share it with. Who could ask for more?"

Kathy, tipping her head to one side, looked over and caught Mack's eye. He gave her an almost imperceptible nod of his head. She broke eye contact. He looked up at the sky and wondered. Lisa took his hand. He knew then, that she asked the right question.

And the answer to it was a simple, *no one could!*